A Practical Guide to Achieving Excellence and High Quality Leadership in Primary Physical Education

association for
Physical
Education

ISBN: 978-1-905540-71-6

Authors:

Merle Hunt, Eileen Marchant and Sue Wilkinson

We extend our thanks and appreciation to the following colleagues who assisted with this publication:

Mark Botterill

Helen Chadwick

Andy Frapwell

John Pearson

Carole Raymond

Keith Spencer

David Turner

Peter Whitlam

afPE appreciates the contributions through review made by:

afPE project lead officer: Sue Wilkinson

Coachwise editor: Abi Masha

Coachwise designer: Carl Heath

Photographs © Alan Edwards

Published on behalf of afPE by

Coachwise Business Solutions

Room 117
Bredon
University of Worcester
Henwick Grove
Worcester
WR2 6AJ
Tel: 01905-855 584
Fax: 01905-855 594

Building 25
London Road
Reading
RG1 5AQ
Tel: 0118-378 2440
Fax: 0118-378 2442
Email: enquiries@afpe.org.uk
Website: www.afpe.org.uk

Coachwise Business Solutions
Chelsea Close
Off Amberley Road, Armley
Leeds LS12 4HP
Tel: 0113-231 1310 Fax: 0113-231 9606
Email:
enquiries@coachwisesolutions.co.uk
Website: www.coachwisesolutions.co.uk

About the authors

Merle Hunt has been a teacher and lecturer of physical education, a local authority and Ofsted inspector for primary and secondary schools. As an education consultant she has worked with numerous agencies including the National Assembly for Wales and several local authorities in England and Wales. She is the author of a range of physical education publications and was project lead officer for many baalpe and afPE publications.

As an Ofsted team inspector, **Eileen Marchant** has undertaken over fifty inspections. She is a lead trainer within the National College for Continuing Professional Development (NCfCPD) and both develops and delivers courses in: teaching and learning, leadership, self evaluation and adults supporting learning (ASL). She is a member of the Professional Development Board for Physical Education and chairs the group responsible for Kitemarking. Until 2005 she was a school improvement officer, responsible for departmental reviews. Eileen is the author of several afPE publications.

Sue Wilkinson was a local authority advisory teacher and an inspector of primary schools for Ofsted and Estyn. She was also Director of Teaching and Learning in an ITTE institution, and is currently Director of the NCfCPD as well as a technical adviser to the Department for Children, Schools and Families (DCSF) and Training Development Agency for Schools (TDA). Sue is the author of various curriculum guidelines and has worked as project lead officer for several baalpe and afPE publications.

Contents

Appendices (downloadable from CD-ROM)

Introduction

A Practical Guide to Achieving Excellence and High Quality Leadership in Primary Physical Education is intended to assist leaders of physical education in primary schools to develop effective high quality physical education in their schools. The idea for the resource is based on the findings of the most recent annual reports from Her Majesty's Inspectorate (HMI) across the UK and current research-based practice. Leadership and management are identified as key areas in need of development, particularly in primary physical education. The constraint of time allocation for physical education within initial teacher training and education (ITTE) for primary teachers, further prevents the development of effective leadership skills in physical education. Although there is much written information about physical education management, there is limited and disparate guidance on effective leadership across all aspects of provision for the subject, particularly at primary level. This resource serves as a practical guide for leaders of physical education to improve their leadership skills. The Association for Physical Education's (afPE) NCfCPD will deliver bespoke continuing professional development (CPD) opportunities to support this resource. According to the TDA's Professional Standards for Teachers (TDA, 2007), all teachers should have a professional responsibility to be engaged in effective, sustained and relevant CPD and should have a contractual entitlement to CPD.

This resource aims to synthesise various government agency strategies, directives and initiatives in order to provide a comprehensive resource for advice, guidance and solutions relating to achieving excellence and high quality leadership. While some leaders of physical education will be managing several subjects, others will be specialists. The objective of this publication is to translate available high quality leadership criteria into practical guidance for achieving effective management of the subject, in order to enhance, extend and enrich physical education provision for all pupils in primary schools. As a starting point for achieving excellence and high quality provision, leaders of physical education need to be very clear about the school's vision for the subject and be committed to making it a reality by:

- designing a physical education curriculum that promotes personal learning and thinking skills
- making sure all pupils are included
- using the time allocation for physical education effectively
- allocating appropriate equipment and accommodation fairly and efficiently
- deploying, supporting and developing teachers effectively
- rewarding and celebrating pupils' achievements appropriately
- monitoring and evaluating pupils' progress and attainment.

The appendices to this publication are in a CD-ROM format. These include exemplar proformas, templates and lists, which are linked to each chapter and aim to assist the practicalities of physical education leadership. They are downloadable in PDF and adaptable Microsoft Word documents.

The resources referenced within this publication are summarised at the end of each chapter. A full list of references is included in Appendix 1.

Teacher Resource Signposts

TDA (2007) 'Professional Standards for Teachers', www.tda.gov.uk/standards

Websites

Association for Physical Education
www.afpe.org.uk

Department for Children, Schools and Families
www.dcsf.gov.uk

Department of Education, Northern Ireland
www.deni.gov.uk

HM Inspectorate for Education and Training in Wales
www.estyn.gov.uk

HM Inspectorate of Education in Scotland
www.hmie.gov.uk

Office for Standards in Education, Children's Services and Skills
www.ofsted.gov.uk

PESS strategy for Wales
www.wales.gov.uk/about/departments/dcells

Qualifications Curriculum Authority
www.qca.org.uk

Training and Development Agency for Schools
www.tda.gov.uk

a practical guide to achieving excellence and high quality leadership in primary physical education

Abbreviations

afPE	The Association for Physical Education
ASL	Adults Supporting Learning
CPD	Continuing Professional Development
CPSU	Child Protection in Sport Unit (NSPCC)
CRB	Criminal Records Bureau (also Disclosure Scotland and AccessNI)
DCMS	Department for Culture, Media and Sport
DCSF	Department for Children, Schools and Families (formerly Department for Education and Skills)
DENI	Department of Education Northern Ireland
EAL	English as an Additional Language
ESTYN	Her Majesty's Inspectorate of Education and Training in Wales
HLTA	Higher Level Teaching Assistant
HMI	Her Majesty's Inspectorate
HMIe	Her Majesty's Inspectorate of Education in Scotland
ICT	Information and Communication Technology
IEP	Individual Educational Plan
ITTE	Initial Teacher Training and Education
LA	Local Authority
NCfCPD	National College for Continuing Professional Development
NCPE	National Curriculum for Physical Education
NGB	National Governing Body
NQT	Newly Qualified Teacher
Ofsted	Office for Standards in Education, Children's Services and Skills
OSHL	Out of School Hours Learning
PSHCE	Personal, Social, Health and Citizenship Education
PDM	Partnership Development Manager
PEITTE	Physical Education Initial Teacher Training and Education
PESS	Physical Education and School Sport
PESSCL	Physical Education and School Sport Club Links
PESSYP	Physical Education and School Sport for Young People
PPA	Planning, Preparation and Assessment
SEN	Special Educational Needs
SENCO	Special Educational Needs Coordinator
SMT	Senior Management Team
SMSC	Spiritual, Moral, Social, Cultural Education
SSCO	School Sport Coordinator
SSPs	School Sport Partnerships
STEP	Space, Task, Equipment, People
TDA	Training and Development Agency for Schools

4

Chapter one

Establishing Excellence and High Quality Leadership in Primary Physical Education

If leaders of physical education are to be effective practitioners, it is essential that there is a clear, consistent and coherent understanding of what high quality physical education is. The Physical Education and School Sport for Young People (PESSYP) strategy target of providing two hours of high quality physical education and school sport (PESS) for all pupils aged 5–16 has largely been met in terms of quantity, but the focus now must be on the quality aspect of that target provision. Additionally, this target has been superseded by the Five Hour Offer, of which two hours of high quality physical education must be in the curriculum. The PESS strategy in Wales has seven core objectives, one of which is to manage the subject effectively within the whole-school curriculum.

When making a judgement about quality, leaders of physical education must be aware of what exactly they are looking for and this should match Ofsted, HM Inspectorates of Education and Training in Wales (Estyn), Scotland (HMIe), the Department of Education Northern Ireland (DENI) and other self-evaluation criteria. When making judgements about the quality of physical education, focus should initially be on:

- Achievement and Standards

- Personal Development and Well-Being.

It is only after considering these aspects that the qualities of contributory factors are evaluated. Thus, when making judgements, it important to use the 10 PESSYP High Quality Outcomes in conjunction with the Ofsted, Estyn, HMIe or DENI inspection framework criteria, because applying the Outcomes in isolation does not provide sufficient detail to make sound judgements.

Achievement and Standards

Five of the PESSYP High Quality Outcomes guide teachers towards what they would expect to see if Achievement and Standards are 'good' or 'better', ie:

- Pupils know and understand what they are trying to achieve.

- Pupils understand that PESS is part of a healthy, active lifestyle.

- Pupils have the skills and control they need.

- Pupils think about what they are doing and make appropriate decisions.

- Pupils have stamina, suppleness and strength.

- Pupils enjoy their work.

The Ofsted criteria for making judgements about high quality Achievement and Standards are as follows:

- Pupils make good progress in skills, knowledge and understanding in all areas of the physical education curriculum.

- Pupils achieve well in comparison to their prior attainment and that of pupils in similar schools.

- Pupils demonstrate good skills, knowledge and understanding in the key processes of physical education and across most areas of activity, with little or nothing that is unsatisfactory in terms of standards.
- Pupils do not underperform in physical education.
- Pupils are involved in school, regional and national teams and/or activities.

Personal Development and Well-Being

The remaining five PESSYP High Quality Outcomes guide teachers towards what they would expect to see if Personal Development and Well-Being are 'good' or 'better':

- Pupils show commitment to PESS.
- Pupils have the confidence to get involved.
- Pupils willingly participate in a range of activities.
- Pupils show a desire to improve and achieve.
- Pupils enjoy PESS.
- Pupils' spiritual, moral, social and cultural (SMSC) development are good.
- Pupils lead healthy lifestyles.

The Ofsted criteria for making judgements about high quality Personal Development and Well-Being are as follows:

- Pupils like physical education and all that it offers.
- Pupils are normally interested in or excited by their work in physical education.
- Pupils are keen to achieve as well as they can in physical education.
- Pupils behave well in physical education lessons and are willing to undertake work of their own accord safely.
- Pupils develop good work-related skills in line with their personal qualities in physical education.
- Pupils respect and value each other, which is demonstrated by their positive attitudes.

Note: Personal Development and Well-Being also link to the five outcomes of Every Child Matters where every child has a right to:

- be healthy
- stay safe
- enjoy and achieve
- make a positive contribution
- achieve economic well-being.

Working with other teachers, leaders of physical education should determine whether physical education is 'outstanding', 'good', 'satisfactory' or 'inadequate'. Any judgement must be backed up with evidence collected from numerous sources, which are identified throughout this publication.

Once judgements have been made about Achievements and Standards and Personal Development and Well-Being, it is then crucial to identify what factors have contributed to these, ie:

- Teaching and Learning
- Curriculum and Other Activities
- Care and Guidance
- Leadership and Management.

Leaders of physical education should provide professional leadership and management to secure 'good' or 'better' in Standards of Achievement and Personal Development and Well-Being for all pupils in their school. In the following chapters, guidance is given about the processes leaders of physical education must establish in order to secure 'good' or 'better' results.

Teacher Resource Signposts

afPE (2006a) *A Guide to Self-review in Physical Education*. Leeds: Coachwise Business Solutions. ISBN: 978-1-902523-98-9

afPE (2006b) *Self-evaluation in Physical Education: Developing the process*. Leeds: Coachwise Business Solutions. ISBN: 978-1-905540-06-8

afPE (2008a) *The Reality of High Quality Physical Education: The Crucial Role of Leadership*. Leeds: Coachwise Business Solutions. ISBN: 978-1-905540-56-3

DCMS/DfES (2004) 'High Quality PE and Sport for Young People', www.teachernet.gov.uk/_doc/6254/HighQualityLeaflet.pdf

DfES (2004) 'Every Child Matters – Change for Children', www.everychildmatters.gov.uk

QCA (2005) 'Do you have high quality PE and sport in your school?', www.qca.org.uk/libraryAssets/media/self_evaluation_guide.pdf

Websites

Department of Education, Northern Ireland
www.deni.gov.uk

HM Inspectorate for Education and Training in Wales
www.estyn.gov.uk

Healthy Schools
www.healthyschools.gov.uk

HM Inspectorate of Education in Scotland
www.hmie.gov.uk

Office for Standards in Education, Children's Services and Skills
www.ofsted.gov.uk

PESS strategy for Wales
www.wales.gov.uk/about/departments/dcells

Chapter two

The Context for Achieving Excellence and High Quality Leadership in Primary Physical Education

2

The Changing Role of Leadership

The principles of effective high quality leadership are well documented. However, during the last five years, it is the extent of physical education leadership that has placed increased demands on primary school teachers. The direction given, and the decisions made, by leaders of physical education have a significant impact on how well pupils will achieve. With increasing demands from a variety of sources, it is important that leaders of physical education focus on the entitlement for all pupils within the National Curriculum. In the absence of nationally agreed subject leader standards, there are inconsistencies in the expectations of teachers who lead physical education.

It is important to recognise that the physical education leader's role is to manage, coach, develop and support other teachers and ASL in their understanding and delivery of physical education within the curriculum. Effective leadership and management are essential to secure high quality teaching, effective use of resources, including information and communication technology (ICT), and improved standards of learning and achievement for all pupils.

The PESS profession in England has welcomed the PESSYP strategy, culminating with the government's aspiration of five hours' PESS. In addition, the following strategies: Every Child Matters, The Children's Plan and the Learning Outside the Classroom manifesto, as well as the changing nature of the school workforce, place great demands on the teacher leading physical education in a primary school. Similarly in Wales, the PESS strategy provides welcome opportunities for pupils; however, it is imperative this initiative is embedded in wider strategies.

This resource draws on the Professional Standards for Teachers (TDA, 2007) in order to identify professional attributes, knowledge and understanding, and skills. It also incorporates five principles from the National College for School Leadership's generic standards, which are:

- leading strategically
- leading teaching and learning
- leading the organisation
- leading people
- leading in the community.

However, leading strategically should be considered fundamental to the successful implementation of the other four principles so leaders of physical education have a clearer understanding of what is expected of them in their role. Thus, the next three chapters of this resource will embed these principles in developing practical exemplification. It is hoped this framework will support leaders of physical education to build a portfolio of evidence that can be used for:

- performance management of PESS professionals
- senior management team (SMT) and governing body accountability
- informing job descriptions and person specifications.

In order to secure the highest levels of achievement and attainment for all pupils, leaders of physical education will be required to take responsibility for selecting, leading and managing an increasingly diverse workforce. Over the last few years, the school workforce has changed dramatically, particularly with the extended use of ASL for planning, preparation and assessment (PPA) time. Extensive guidance exists on the employment, deployment and management of volunteers and coaches in PESS, such as that provided by the DCSF, NSPCC Child Protection in Sport Unit (CPSU) and afPE.

However, the main focus of attention should be to ensure that the curriculum enables all pupils to build on prior learning, experience a broad and balanced entitlement to learning and experience a smooth transition through their key stages. In addition, leaders of physical education should also manage a high quality curriculum for all pupils with explicit opportunities for physical education and cross-curricular studies so that pupils use and apply their developing subject knowledge, skills and understanding.

Teacher Resource Signposts

afPE (2008b) *Safe Practice in Physical Education and School Sport*. Leeds: Coachwise Business Solutions. ISBN: 978-1-905540-54-9

afPE (2007b) *Professional Development Record*. Leeds: Coachwise Business Solutions. ISBN: 978-1-905540-39-6

afPE/sports coach UK (2007) *Adults Supporting Learning (including Coaches and Volunteers): A framework for development*. Leeds: Coachwise Business Solutions. ISBN: 978-1-905540-28-0

CfSA Primary Subjects (2009) 'Physical Education: Learning outside the classroom', www.afpe.org.uk/public/downloads/Pri_sub_4.pdf

DCMS/DfES (2004) 'High Quality PE and Sport for Young People', www.teachernet.gov.uk/_doc/6254/HighQualityLeaflet.pdf

DCSF (2004) 'Every Child Matters – Change for Children', www.everychildmatters.gov.uk

DCSF (2006) 'Learning Outside the Classroom', www.lotc.org.uk/getmedia/b84de479-7990-482c-a17b-b527ae7d32f2/LOtC-Leaflet.aspx

DCSF (2007) 'The Children's Plan: Building Brighter Futures', www.dcsf.gov.uk/childrensplan

TDA (2007) 'Professional Standards for Teachers', www.tda.gov.uk/standards

Websites

Association for Physical Education
www.afpe.org.uk

Council for Subject Associations
www.subjectassociations.org.uk

Learning Outside the Classroom
www.lotc.org.uk

National College for School Leadership
www.ncsl.org.uk

NSPCC Child Protection in Sport Unit
www.nspcc.org.uk/inform/cpsu/cpsu_wda57648.html

PESS strategy for Wales
www.wales.gov.uk/about/departments/dcells

PESSYP Professional Development Programme
www.youthsporttrust.org/page/cpd/index.html

---

a practical guide to achieving excellence and high quality leadership in primary physical education

Chapter three

3

Professional Attributes for Achieving Excellence and High Quality Leadership in Primary Physical Education

This chapter focuses on physical education exemplification of the generic 'Professional Attributes' standards identified in the Professional Standards for Teachers (TDA, 2007), together with the following principles of the National College for School Leadership:

- leading strategically
- leading teaching and learning
- leading the organisation
- leading people.

The effective **strategic** leader of physical education operates:

- with pupils, leading people:
  - as a class teacher
  - as a specialist
  - as a point of reference

- with teachers and other adults, leading teaching and learning, and leading people:
  - as an adviser, mentor, specialist
  - as a provider of teaching and learning resources
  - as a CPD source

- with the school, leading people/leading in the community:
  - as a resource for curriculum development
  - as an advocate for physical education for a variety of stakeholders
  - as an author for curriculum guidelines and policies
  - as a designer and person to monitor the assessment for learning policy
  - as the point of reference for partnership schools.

The key to unlocking the full potential of pupils and ensuring they experience a wide range of personal, social and emotional attributes, essential to their health and well-being for life as responsible citizens in the 21st century, lies in the expertise and effectiveness of PESS professionals.

There are four identified types of leadership (*Achieving Excellence*, baalpe, 2003):

1. Visionary – where leadership depends on leaders of physical education having a vision about where the future of physical education lies and how to develop the vision within the whole school.

2. Impact – where leadership calls upon the leader of physical education to make a difference through promoting the subject and engendering enthusiasm for it through being a good role model that includes integrity, creativity and imagination.

3. Strategic – where leadership arises out of the application of accumulated knowledge, experience and understanding of the physical education curriculum, resulting in planning and delivery that is systematic, progressive and dynamic.

4. Interpersonal – where leadership relies upon the leader of physical education having the skills and attributes to ensure effective communication (both within and outside of the subject) of the ethos, standards, importance and significance of physical education within the school and, where appropriate, to enthuse others to follow.

Elements of all four of these leadership styles are clearly evident in the exemplification below and they are inextricably linked. For example, visionary leadership could be determining what high quality physical education looks like. Impact leadership could be establishing what the leader of physical education needs to do in order to achieve high quality leadership. Strategic leadership could be establishing the strategies to achieve high quality physical education. Interpersonal leadership could be determining the competence and suitability of staff to achieve high quality physical education. The critical factor is for leaders to adopt a balanced approach.

As a result of leaders setting and implementing consistent policies across the PESS workforce, pupils will know and understand what is expected of them. The physical education leader will, through effective communication, ensure the subject is valued and respected by all stakeholders so that pupils will value the contribution physical education, health and personal well-being can make to their lifestyles. The PESS workforce should deliver the subject to the same high standards to achieve the most effective outcomes for all pupils. By constantly reviewing the workforce's knowledge, skills and understanding of physical education, pupils should receive a high quality education. The physical education leader must monitor the workforce's professional development to ensure high quality provision is maintained.

Exemplification of the TDA's 'Professional Attributes' Standards for High Quality Leadership in Primary Physical Education

Criteria All leaders in physical education should:	Evidence What does it look like?	Exemplification – Practical Examples Ideas for implementation

1. Relationship with pupils
 	
1.1 Have high expectations.
 	
1.2 Demonstrate appropriate and high professional standards.
	• Leader is a model of good practice in relation to teaching.
	
	• Leader sets high standards and he/she inspires others.
	
	• Leader sets relevant tasks for all pupils.
	
	• Leader leads by example to staff and pupils.
	
	• Leader conducts him/herself in a professional manner with all stakeholders.
	
	• School is held in high respect within the community.
		• Staff should always be appropriately dressed.
		
		• Planning documents should be well prepared and meticulous, see:
		
		  ▪ *Appendix 9: Primary Lesson Plans*
		
		  ▪ *Appendix 10: The STEP Process.*
		
		• School to be well publicised and respected by the community and features positively in local newsletters.
		
		• Pupils should always be well equipped and prepared for physical education. For policies on clothing, refer to:
		
		  ▪ *Safe Practice in Physical Education and School Sport* (afPE, 2008b).

Criteria All leaders in physical education should:	Evidence What does it look like?	Exemplification – Practical Examples Ideas for implementation
2. Frameworks 2.1 Take a strategic lead in developing relevant workplace policies and ensuring implementation in the workplace.	• Provision runs smoothly on a day-to-day basis. • All policies are regularly monitored and reviewed. • Provision and policies are implemented consistently. • Support is provided to those who require further understanding of how to implement the policies. • Good teamwork and collaboration is evident.	• Minutes of meetings should reflect discussion and review of policies. • Regular staff updates and bulletins, focusing on raising achievement, should be distributed. • Minutes of SMT meetings should reflect education focus. • Regular one-to-one meetings with staff should be well documented and recorded.
3. Communicating and working with others 3.1 Communicate effectively with all stakeholders. 3.2 Recognise and respect the contributions that all colleagues and other adults can make to the development and well-being of young people. 3.3 Be committed to collaboration and cooperative working. 3.4 Be a lead advocate for physical education.	• Leader is innovative, knowledgeable and has a strategic view. • Vision for improvement is communicated clearly with enthusiasm. • Messages are clearly conveyed in meetings, written communication and school events. • Subject documentation is accurate and up to date. • Teachers and other professionals are deployed appropriately and effectively to the curriculum and Out of School Hours Learning (OSHL). • ASL and volunteers to support teachers are deployed effectively. • Parents and carers are actively engaged with to ensure they know and understand pupils' development. • Leader manages attractive and up-to-date areas for physical education. • Success stories within physical education are promoted. • SMT and other staff are regularly updated on developments within physical education.	• Minutes and action notes of meetings should be made available to all staff. • School events should be publicised throughout the school, community and in local press. • All personnel should be involved within and outside of the curriculum and in meetings, see: ▪ *Appendix 4: Best-practice Guidance on the Effective Use of Individual and Agency Coaches in PESS.* • ASL should be present in meetings and/or have copies of communications. • Pupils should see the entire workforce as PESS professionals and not treat ASL differently to teachers. • Parents and carers should attend school events within and outside of the curriculum. • Physical education areas should be well maintained and motivating. • News stories and email bulletins should be sent to staff and community about PESS successes. • Albums and scrapbooks should be readily available for the community/visitors.

Criteria All leaders in physical education should:	Evidence What does it look like?	Exemplification – Practical Examples Ideas for implementation
	• Pupils and physical education are promoted within the local community.	• Pictures and editorials should be featured in the local press and on parents' and carers' noticeboards.
4. Personal professional development 4.1 Evaluate their own and others, performance. 4.2 Be effective coaches and mentors. 4.3 Be researchers and evaluators of innovative curricular practices. 4.4 Draw on research outcomes from other sources of external evidence to inform their own practice and that of colleagues.	• Leadership has a clear vision for improvement focused on high quality outcomes. • Ensuring accurate and regular staff observations and self-reviews are carried out. • CPD is promoted in physical education for all colleagues and the impact on pupils' learning is monitored. • Impact of leadership is evident in good progress made by pupils. • Teachers demonstrate good understanding of strengths and areas for development through effective self-evaluation. • Teachers and other professionals know what is expected of them. • Teamwork is actively promoted among all PESS personnel.	• Staff documentation should include procedures for self-review and targets for improvement. Refer to: ▪ TDA Performance Management web page ▪ *Professional Development Record* (afPE, 2007b). • Peer-observation sessions are timetabled for lesson-observation guidance and proformas, see: ▪ *Appendix 12: Protocols for Observing Lessons* ▪ *Appendix 14: Suggested Questions to Ask When Sharing Lesson Observations* ▪ *Appendix 15: Examples of Lesson Observation Proformas* ▪ *Appendix 16: Feedback Proforma.* • Timetabled CPD opportunities. For CPD proforma, see: ▪ *Appendix 22: PESS CPD Audit of Needs Example Proformas.* Also refer to: ▪ *Self-evaluation in Physical Education: Developing the process* (afPE, 2006b) ▪ *A Guide to Self-review in Physical Education* (afPE, 2006a). • Strategies are in place for recording and sharing feedback from CPD opportunities. • Physical education meetings include peer observation and moderation. • Minutes demonstrate engagement in professional debate about improving performance to raise standards.

14

Criteria All leaders in physical education should:	Evidence What does it look like?	Exemplification – Practical Examples Ideas for implementation
		• ASL have opportunities for observing effective teaching and learning. • Staff share up-to-date research, see: ▪ physical education ITTE (PEITTE) website.

Teacher Resource Signposts

afPE (2006a) *A Guide to Self-review in Physical Education*. Leeds: Coachwise Business Solutions. ISBN: 978-1-902523-98-9

afPE (2006b) *Self-evaluation in Physical Education: Developing the process*. Leeds: Coachwise Business Solutions. ISBN: 978-1-905540-06-8

afPE (2007b) *Professional Development Record*. Leeds: Coachwise Business Solutions. ISBN: 978-1-905540-39-6

afPE (2008b) *Safe Practice in Physical Education and School Sport*. Leeds: Coachwise Business Solutions. ISBN: 978-1-905540-54-9

afPE/sports coach UK (2007) *Adults Supporting Learning (including Coaches and Volunteers): A framework for development*. Leeds: Coachwise Business Solutions. ISBN: 978-1-905540-28-0

baalpe (2003) *Achieving Excellence*. Leeds: Coachwise Business Solutions. ISBN: 1-902523-57-1

TDA (2007) 'Professional Standards for Teachers', www.tda.gov.uk/standards

Websites

Association for Physical Education
www.afpe.org.uk

Coachwise 1st4sport
www.1st4sport.com

National College for School Leadership
www.ncsl.org.uk

PEITTE Website
www.peitte.net

PESS strategy for Wales
www.wales.gov.uk/about/departments/dcells

Training and Development Agency for Schools
www.tda.gov.uk

TDA Performance Management
www.tda.gov.uk/teachers/performance_management.aspx

a practical guide to achieving excellence and high quality leadership in primary physical education

Chapter four

Professional Knowledge and Understanding for Achieving Excellence and High Quality Leadership in Primary Physical Education

4

This chapter focuses on physical education exemplification of the generic 'Professional Knowledge and Understanding' standards identified in Professional Standards for Teachers (TDA, 2007), together with the following principles of the National College for School Leadership:

- leading strategically
- leading teaching and learning
- leading the organisation
- leading people.

A clear grasp of the nature of physical education is paramount if the subject is to be led effectively and given sufficient emphasis within the curriculum to ensure a balanced provision for all pupils. Physical education is exposed to curricular pressure in primary schools and is sometimes shaped by traditional expectations or teacher preference rather than the explicit needs of pupils. Where diverse interpretations occur, they weaken what should be a common and effective learning experience for all pupils. The leadership, direction and decisions made by the leader of physical education have a significant impact on how well pupils achieve.

Effective leaders of physical education should instigate working collaboratively with all teachers and ASL in the school in order to raise standards in physical education. A common sense of purpose is thus created among staff. Critical understanding of the most effective teaching, learning and behaviour-management strategies will help support personalised, compelling learning opportunities in order to achieve individual potential. High quality leadership is dependent on the ability to master the conceptual structure of physical education, adopt a range of appropriate approaches to teaching and keep up to date with current developments in the subject. Therefore, the key issue is to inspire and support other teachers in the school in delivering the planned physical education programme effectively.

Leaders of physical education need to ensure that all teachers and other PESS professionals are familiar with the assessment arrangements for physical education, that they know how to improve their practice for individuals and how to develop effective use of assessment as an integral part of their teaching. This is fundamental in achieving high quality physical education provision and will assist in diagnosing and meeting pupils' needs by setting appropriate challenges and clear learning targets.

Leaders of physical education are obligated to design and establish a purposeful physical education curriculum that promotes effective learning. This will involve an understanding of, and compliance with, current legal requirements and national policies and guidance on the safeguarding and well-being of pupils if they are to feel secure and sufficiently confident to make an active contribution to learning and to the school. Care should be taken to ensure that leaders' expert knowledge and understanding of physical education is shared to develop the PESS workforce. Together, they should not only plan a corporate physical education curriculum that takes note of progression across the range of age and ability, but should also identify and explore links with cross-curricular dimensions. The resulting documentation should then provide effective learning sequences within lessons as well as across a series of lessons.

Exemplification of the TDA's 'Professional Knowledge and Understanding' Standards for High Quality Leadership in Primary Physical Education

Criteria All leaders in physical education should:	Evidence What does it look like?	Exemplification – Practical Examples Ideas for implementation

1. Teaching and learning
 	
1.1 Have a good knowledge and critical understanding of a range of teaching, learning and behaviour-management strategies, knowing how to use and adapt them as well as how to personalise learning and provide opportunities for all learners to achieve their potential.
	• All learners make good progress throughout the school as a result of effective teaching.
	
	• All teachers demonstrate good subject knowledge.
	
	• Teachers use a range of appropriate teaching approaches to engage learners and encourage independent work.
	
	• Learners are stretched through appropriate challenges that do not inhibit learning.
	
	• All work tailored to the full range of learners' needs is successful.
	
	• Challenging, well organised lessons and sequences of lessons are taught across the age and ability range.
	
	• Tasks are relevant and challenging and match learners' diverse needs, including the gifted and talented as well as those with special educational needs (SEN).
	
	• An appropriate range of teaching approaches, language and resources is used that meets individual pupils' needs.
	
	• Teaching builds on current knowledge and attainment levels of individual pupils in order to meet identified learning objectives and make sustained progress.
		• Refer to:
		
		  ▪ *Appendix 7: Teaching Styles and Preferred Learning Styles*
		
		  ▪ *The Reality of High Quality Physical Education: The Crucial Role of Leadership* (afPE, 2008a).
		
		• Appropriate CPD for all staff should be identified and linked to performance management, see:
		
		  ▪ TDA Performance Management web page
		
		  ▪ *Professional Development Record* (afPE, 2007b).
		
		• Team teaching and observation of lessons can be helpful to develop teaching and learning aspects and consistency in standards. This can initially be managed via appropriate DVD observation, see:
		
		  ▪ *Self-evaluation in Physical Education: Developing the process* (afPE, 2006b) for DVD observation of primary lessons.
		
		• Staff should be mindful of sensitivities involved in observing lessons – see
		
		  ▪ *Appendix 12: Protocols for Observing Lessons.*
		
		• For consistency and sharing of criteria for judging teaching and learning, see:
		
		  ▪ *Appendix 13: Evaluation of Teaching*
		
		  ▪ *Appendix 23: Inclusion Spectrum for PESS*
		
		  ▪ *Every Child Matters: Measuring Moments of Progress and Inclusive Assessment* (afPE, 2007a).

Criteria All leaders in physical education should:	Evidence What does it look like?	Exemplification – Practical Examples Ideas for implementation

	• The learning of pupils as individuals, groups and whole classes is managed effectively and teaching is modified appropriately to suit the lesson and needs of pupils.
	
	• Teaching is engaging and motivates behaviour positively and effectively.
	
	• Lessons are informed by well-grounded expectations of pupils and designed to raise levels of attainment.
		• For examples of lesson observation proformas and feedback forms, see:
		  ▪ *Appendix 15: Examples of Lesson Proformas*
		  ▪ *Appendix 16: Feedback Proforma*
		  ▪ 'Simple Guide to Completing your Self-evaluation Form' (afPE, 2008c).
		
		• For suggested questions to ask when giving feedback lesson observations, see:
		  ▪ *Appendix 14: Suggested Questions to Ask When Sharing Lesson Observations.*
		
		• Where funding is provided for staff cover, some should be used to develop structured lesson observations.

2. Assessment and monitoring
 	
2.1 Know the assessment requirements and arrangements for physical education and know how to help teachers improve the effectiveness of their assessment practice.
 	
2.2 Know a range of approaches to assessment, including the importance of formative assessment.
 	
2.3 Know how to analyse and use local and national statistical information to
	• Thorough and accurate assessment that informs learners how to improve.
	
	• Learners are guided to assess work themselves.
	
	• Good diagnosis is evident in matching work and approaches to those with individual learning needs.
	
	• An appropriate range of observation, assessment, monitoring and recording strategies is used as a basis for setting challenging learning objectives and for monitoring pupils' progress and levels of attainment.
	
	• Pupils, teachers, parents and carers are provided with timely, accurate and constructive feedback on pupils' attainment, progress and areas for development.
	
	• Pupils are supported and guided so they can reflect on their learning, identify the progress
		• Ensure effective transition strategies are in place for each key stage and from year to year. Refer to:
		  ▪ *Assessment for Learning in Physical Education* (afPE, 2005)
		
		• When planning for improvement, progress and attainment, QCA core tasks should be used to establish a baseline for appropriate tasks, adapting or modifying as appropriate. See:
		  ▪ *Appendix 5: The National Curriculum for Physical Education (NCPE)'s Three Principles for Inclusion*
		  ▪ *Every Child Matters: Measuring Moments of Progress and Inclusive Assessment* (afPE, 2007)
		  ▪ *Success for All: An Inclusive Approach to PE and School Sport* (DfES, 2003)
		  ▪ 'Primary and Secondary Inclusion Development Programme – Supporting

| Criteria | Evidence | Exemplification – |
| All leaders in physical education should: | What does it look like? | Practical Examples |
		Ideas for implementation
evaluate the effectiveness of teaching, monitor the progress of those they teach and raise levels of attainment. 2.4 Know how to use reports and other sources of external information related to assessment in order to provide learners with accurate and constructive feedback on their strengths, weaknesses, attainment, progress and areas for development, including action plans for improvement.	they have made, set positive targets for improvement and become successful independent learners. • Using assessment as an integral part of teaching to diagnose pupils' needs in order to set realistic and challenging targets for improvement and to plan future learning.	pupils on the autism spectrum' (DCSF, 2009) ■ 'Meeting the Needs of Muslim Pupils in State Schools' (Birmingham CYPF/ Birmingham University, 2008). • Ensure that all staff, accommodation and resources are deployed effectively to enhance learning. For self-evaluation proformas, see: ■ *Appendix 19: Monitoring the Adequacy and Suitability of Physical Education Staff* ■ *Appendix 20: Monitoring the Efficiency of How Equipment, Learning Resources and Accommodation are Managed to Ensure Pupils are Well Taught and Protected.* • Assessment should take note of up-to-date and accurate records, developed over time through discussions, observations, planning and evaluations, including: ■ observation of learners at work in lessons, playgrounds extra-curricular activities and activities beyond the school (see *Appendix 21: Primary Playgrounds Development/ Sporting Playgrounds Poster*) ■ attendance and participation records in physical education lessons ■ discussions with pupils, other teachers, parents, assistant teachers and other ASL ■ targets set compared with targets achieved ■ transfer of information from previous school/class ■ assessment for learning information in planning and lesson observations

Criteria All leaders in physical education should:	Evidence What does it look like?	Exemplification – Practical Examples Ideas for implementation
		<ul><li>use of core tasks to determine progress</li><li>learners' own assessments</li><li>pupils' written work.</li></ul>
3. Subjects and curriculum 3.1 Have a competent and secure knowledge and understanding of physical education and related pedagogy, including the contribution that physical education can make to cross-curricular learning to enable effective teaching across the age and ability range for which they have trained. 3.2 Know and understand the relevant statutory and non-statutory framework, including other relevant initiatives applicable to the age and ability range for which they have trained.	<ul><li>Statutory requirements are met to provide a broad and balanced physical education curriculum for **all** pupils.</li><li>Curriculum is responsive to local needs.</li><li>Learners have the opportunity to take responsibility.</li><li>Curriculum enables all learners to progress and develop well through clear, well-sequenced learning outcomes.</li><li>Establishing clear progression routes through learning stages.</li><li>Good-quality enrichment opportunities are varied enjoyed and have a high take-up.</li></ul>	<ul><li>Refer to:<ul><li>QCA physical education statutory guidance on National Curriculum website</li><li>'Statutory Inclusion Statement' (QCA, 1999).</li></ul></li><li>Clear links should be identified with areas across the curriculum (eg PSHCE, SMSC, key skills, literacy, numeracy and ICT) within planning documents. See:<ul><li>*Appendix 6: Learning Across the Curriculum*</li><li>Healthy Schools website.</li></ul></li><li>Cross curricular and links to Every Child Matters should be identified in medium- and short-term plans. Refer to:<ul><li>'Physical Education: Making Every Child Matter' (CfSA Primary Subjects, 2008).</li></ul></li><li>Appropriate opportunities should be provided for measuring, data analysis and recording.</li><li>Policies and procedures should be in place and monitored and evaluated for:<ul><li>attendance/participation</li><li>child protection</li><li>risk management</li><li>health and safety policy</li><li>reporting to parents/carers.</li></ul>Refer to:<ul><li>*Safe Practice in Physical Education and School Sport* (afPE, 2008b)</li><li>Health and safety updates and NCfCPD opportunities on afPE website.</li></ul></li></ul>

Criteria All leaders in physical education should:	Evidence What does it look like?	Exemplification – Practical Examples Ideas for implementation
4. Literacy, numeracy and ICT 4.1 Know how to use skills in literacy, numeracy and ICT to support their teaching and wider professional activities.	• Good provision is evident for literacy, numeracy and ICT throughout the school, for all subjects and all pupils. • Maximising effective opportunities whereby the PESS workforce embed literacy, numeracy and ICT in the physical education curriculum.	• Use methods that engage pupils' thirst for new technology, which can also be applied to physical education lessons and the battle against obesity. • Use cost-effective resources to compile films and photographic images of pupils engaged in sporting activity for analysis and development. • Analyse digital photographs and video footage of sporting performances to assess techniques, evaluate style and pinpoint areas for future improvement. • Show pupils what they have achieved from the beginning to the end of term so they can then understand the true value of physical education. • "ICT provides us with the opportunity to raise standards in our lessons. We can say this is what we're working towards, this is your goal, let's do it better." PESS strategy for Wales, March 2005. • Use the Internet to access information. • Use ICT to measure or evaluate performance. • Review and evaluate performance, using digital tools.

5. Achievement and diversity
 	
5.1 Understand how pupils develop and that the progress and well-being of learners are affected by a range of developmental, social, religious, ethnic, cultural and linguistic influences.
	• The progress of the great majority of learners, in skills, knowledge and understanding, is good in all areas of the physical education curriculum.
	
	• Few learners underperform in physical education.
	
	• Individual achievement is celebrated through a reward system that motivates and inspires all pupils, so that they feel successful and valued.
		• Make sure activities are differentiated using STEP, teaching styles are varied and activities are undertaken alone, in pairs and in small groups or teams, see:
		
		  ▪ *Appendix 10: The STEP Process*
		  ▪ afPE website.
		
		• Inclusive practice should be evident in all planning documents, see:
		
		  ▪ *Appendix 8: How Teaching Styles and Preferred Learning Styles Can Be Addressed in*

a practical guide to achieving excellence and high quality leadership in primary physical education

Criteria All leaders in physical education should:	Evidence What does it look like?	Exemplification – Practical Examples Ideas for implementation
5.2 Know how to make effective personalised provision for all pupils, including those for whom English is an additional language (EAL) or who have SEN or disabilities. Also, know how to take practical account of diversity and promote equality and inclusion in their teaching. 5.3 Know when and how to draw on the expertise of others, such as those with responsibility for safeguarding pupils, and SEN and disabilities; and to refer to sources of information, advice and support from external agencies.	• Promoting inclusivity in all aspects of physical education delivery. • 100% participation in lessons is evident across the whole age, ability, cultural and gender spectrum. • A varied range of resources is well used to improve learning outcomes. • Effective screening and diagnosis of needs and preferred learning styles matches work to those with additional learning needs. • All work tailored to the full range of individual learners' needs is successful. • A directory of all external agency personnel and ASL is coordinated through the special educational needs coordinator (SENCO).	*Planning Documents* ■ *Appendix 9: Primary Lesson Plans* ■ *Appendix 23: Inclusion Spectrum for PESS* ■ *Success for All: An Inclusive Approach to PE and School Sport (DfES, 2003)* ■ *'Primary and Secondary Inclusion Development Programme – Supporting pupils on the autism spectrum' (DCSF, 2009)* ■ *'Meeting the Needs of Muslim Pupils In State Schools' (Birmingham CYPF/Birmingham University, 2008).* • Resources and teaching styles should take cognisance of the individual preferred learning styles/needs of pupils, see: ■ *Appendix 8: How Teaching Styles and Preferred Learning Styles Can Be Addressed in Planning Documents* ■ *Appendix 9: Primary Lesson Plans* ■ Reinforce concepts through different senses (eg touch, sight, hearing). • Seek appropriate use of ASL for specific learners, see: ■ *Appendix 4: Best-practice Guidance on the Effective Use of Individual and Agency Coaches* ■ *Every Child Matters: Measuring Moments of Progress and Inclusive Assessment (afPE, 2007a)* for an assessment framework for pupils aged 5–16 years who are unable to attain age-related expected levels.

Criteria All leaders in physical education should:	Evidence What does it look like?	Exemplification – Practical Examples Ideas for implementation
		▪ Use individual educational plans (IEPs) to support individualised learning. • Set up a support/protocol group with a range of appropriate adults and agencies supporting learners (eg physiotherapists, SENCO, coaches, local authority (LA) inclusion officer, parents, child-protection officers, ethnic/cultural groups), in supporting individuals' progress and learning needs, see: ▪ *Appendix 11: Best-practice Case Study.* • Ensure that a robust screening procedure is in place for early identification of specific learning needs or disabilities, see: ▪ *Appendix 5: The NCPE's Three Principles for Inclusion.*
6. Health and well-being 6.1 Be aware of current legal requirements, national policies and guidance on the safeguarding and promotion of the well-being of pupils. 6.2 Know how to identify and support pupils whose progress, development or well-being is affected by changes or difficulties in their personal circumstances, and when to refer them to colleagues for specialist support.	• Learners like physical education and take part in all that it offers. • Playtimes are friendly and safe. • Learners respect and value each other and this is demonstrated by their positive attitudes. • Good staff commitment to, and competence in, promoting health and well-being. • Child-protection issues are robust (eg Criminal Records Bureau [CRB] checks for coaches/ASL). • Social and emotional well-being is monitored and supported. • All pupils demonstrate a good awareness and understanding of personal health and well-being and	• It is imperative that up-to-date social and emotional policies are established, monitored and reviewed. • Schools should establish safe, well-supervised playgrounds which are exciting and challenging, with diverse areas for girls, boys and those who wish to have quieter moments, see: ▪ *Appendix 21: Primary Playgrounds Development/ Sporting Playgrounds Poster.* • Older pupils could be trained as playground leaders/buddies. • Pupils could develop a 'fair play' charter based on respect and tolerance of others. • A good understanding of pupils' normal behaviour is critical in order to identify dramatic changes that might underpin instability in their social or emotional state.

Criteria All leaders in physical education should:	Evidence What does it look like?	Exemplification – Practical Examples Ideas for implementation
	of the importance of regular physical activity. • Pupils feel safe from bullying or racism. • Pupils have confidence to talk to staff and others if and when they feel at risk. • Pupils express their views well and take part in communal activities.	• CRB checks should be in place and up to date. • ASL should undertake a physical-awareness course and teachers should be aware of their duties and responsibilities when working with ASL. Refer to: • *Adults Supporting Learning (including Coaches and Volunteers): A framework for development* (afPE/sports coach UK, 2007) • afPE NCfCPD website • Healthy Schools website.

Teacher Resource Signposts

afPE (2005) *Assessment for Learning in Physical Education*. Leeds: Coachwise Business Solutions. ISBN: 978-1-902523-79-2

afPE (2006b) *Self-evaluation in Physical Education: Developing the process*. Leeds: Coachwise Business Solutions. ISBN: 978-1-905540-06-8

afPE (2007a) *Every Child Matters: Measuring Moments of Progress and Inclusive Assessment*. Leeds: Coachwise Business Solutions. ISBN: 978-1-905540-40-2

afPE (2007b) *Professional Development Record*. Leeds: Coachwise Business Solutions. ISBN: 978-1-905540-39-6

afPE (2008a) *The Reality of High Quality Physical Education: The Crucial Role of Leadership*. Leeds: Coachwise Business Solutions. ISBN: 978-1-905540-56-3

afPE (2008b) *Safe Practice in Physical Education and School Sport*. Leeds: Coachwise Business Solutions. ISBN: 978-1-905540-54-9

afPE (2008c) 'Simple Guide to Completing your Self Evaluation Form', www.afpe.org.uk/public/downloads/SEF_guide.doc

afPE/sports coach UK (2007) *Adults Supporting Learning (including Coaches and Volunteers): A framework for development*. Leeds: Coachwise Business Solutions. ISBN: 978-1-905540-28-0

Birmingham CYPF/University of Birmingham (2008) 'Meeting the Needs of Muslim Pupils in State Schools', www.afpe.org.uk/public/downloads/muslim_guidance_nov08.pdf

CfSA Primary Subjects (2008) 'Physical Education: Making every child matter', www.afpe.org.uk/public/downloads/CfSA_PE_Apr08.pdf

DCSF (2009) 'Primary and Secondary Inclusion Development Programme – Supporting pupils on the autism spectrum', http://nationalstrategies.standards.dcsf.gov.uk/node/165037

DfES (2003) *Success for All: An Inclusive Approach to PE and School Sport* (CD-ROM). DfES: 054 2003

QCA (1999) 'Statutory Inclusion Statement', http://curriculum.qca.org.uk/key-stages-1-and-2/inclusion/statutory-inclusion-statement/index.aspx

TDA (2007) 'Professional Standards for Teachers', www.tda.gov.uk/standards

Websites

Association for Physical Education
www.afpe.org.uk

Coachwise 1st4sport
www.1st4sport.com

Council for Subject Associations
www.subjectassociations.org.uk

Criminal Records Bureau
www.crb.gov.uk

Department for Children, Schools and Families
www.dcsf.gov.uk

Healthy Schools
www.healthyschools.gov.uk

National College for Continuing Professional Development
www.afpe.org.uk/public/ncfcpd_courses.htm

National Curriculum
http://curriculum.qca.org.uk/

PESS strategy for Wales
www.wales.gov.uk/about/departments/dcells

TDA Performance Management
www.tda.gov.uk/teachers/performance_management.aspx

a practical guide to achieving excellence and high quality leadership in primary physical education

Chapter five

Professional Skills for Achieving Excellence and High Quality Leadership in Primary Physical Education

5

This chapter focuses on the physical education exemplification of the generic professional skills standards identified in the Professional Standards for Teachers (TDA, 2007) together with the following principles outlined by the National College for School Leadership:

- leading strategically

- leading teaching and learning

- leading the organisation

- leading people

- leading the community.

Leaders of physical education should ensure all appropriate PESS personnel are well informed about, and involved in, compiling physical education policies, plans and priorities. Levels of success in meeting objectives and targets, and professional development plans, should be evaluated at regularly planned intervals. It is especially important that leaders support teachers and other professionals to plan effectively so that pupils make good progress through each unit of work and through the key stage or phase, in order for all pupils to achieve well.

Leaders should also have a good overview of how physical education links to other subjects and how the subject supports the achievement of the five outcomes of Every Child Matters. Planning should identify how these links are to be developed and there should be ongoing monitoring of the impact on learning as a result of these links.

Leaders should create a climate that enables teachers and other professionals to develop and maintain positive attitudes towards physical education, and their confidence in teaching it. This should be done through having effective agreed strategies for managing behaviour through effective teaching and learning. Time given for PPA should be well managed so a consistent approach is developed across the subject.

Effective leaders in physical education identify and provide appropriate CPD so that teachers and other professionals keep up to date with current practices, such as assessing pupil progress. Agreed targets, which are sufficiently challenging, should ensure that all pupils achieve according to their ability and prior learning.

Leaders of physical education should develop and implement policies and practices for physical education that reflect the school's commitment to high achievement and good personal development and well-being through effective teaching and learning. Systems should be in place that provide time for teachers and other professionals to self-review as well as time for observation, team teaching and appraisal.

Leaders are also responsible for ensuring appropriate risk-management procedures are in place to ensure all pupils are safe. These should link into whole-school policies as well as advice and guidance from the LA, and that found in *Safe Practice in Physical Education and School Sport* (afPE 2008b). The safeguarding and well-being of pupils should always be given priority in all areas of activity.

Leaders should identify and make use of opportunities outside of school and in the community so that pupils can enrich and enhance their learning opportunities in the curriculum. Collaborative activities in families of schools within school sport partnerships (SSPs) should be maximised so all pupils can access wider learning outside of the school.

A leader in physical education should not only promote team working and collaboration within the context of physical education, but should also be part of, or linked to, the leadership team. The link between whole-school policies and practices is crucial if high quality physical education is to be achieved for all pupils. Links outside of school through SSP are also essential as part of the high quality agenda.

Exemplification of the TDA's 'Professional Skills' Standards for High Quality Leadership in Primary Physical Education

Criteria All leaders in physical education should:	Evidence What does it look like?	Exemplification – Practical Examples Ideas for implementation
1. Planning 1.1 Take a lead in planning collaboratively with colleagues to raise standards by ensuring there is planned progression across the age and ability range. 1.2. Ensure that links with other subjects are identified and planned for.	• Planning and ongoing reviewing and evaluating of the impact on pupils' learning is carried out after each lesson and at the end of each unit of work. • Differentiation is planned for so that all pupils can make good progress. • Teachers keep their own detailed planning file within the school's common planning format. • Teachers demonstrate good understanding of progression in physical education. • Planning is progressive and each unit of work links to previous units. • Cross-curricular links are identified in planning documents. • Learning across the curriculum, including links to Every Child Matters is highlighted in planning documents.	• Time should be given for staff to meet and work collaboratively when planning in year groups in small schools, across the key stage. • An agreement is needed as to how schemes are implemented and how progression is ensured through year groups and key stages. • Schemes should provide ideas for content, but should only be used as planning tools to ensure inclusion and appropriate progression are addressed. For examples of planning formats, see: ▪ *Appendix 8: How Teaching Styles and Preferred Learning Styles Can Be Addressed in Planning Documents* ▪ *Appendix 9: Primary Lesson Plans.* • Long-term planning needs to map NCPE across year groups and key stages, to ensure a broad and balanced curriculum that meets statutory requirements in terms of range and content. • Medium-term planning should identify clear learning objectives, which are linked to key skills and processes of the NCPE as well as the content of what is to be learnt.

Criteria All leaders in physical education should:	Evidence What does it look like?	Exemplification – Practical Examples Ideas for implementation
		• Short-term planning by individual teachers should be carried out weekly. • Short-term learning outcomes should link to the medium-term ones. The content (ie what is to be learnt) should be clearly identified. • Cross curricular and links to Every Child Matters should be identified in medium- and short-term plans (eg ICT should be used to enhance learning, such as the use of digital equipment to enable pupils to evaluate their work). The Internet can also be used to access information about health and well-being. • Opportunities for speaking and listening should be planned for in each lesson in groups and paired work. Where topics and themes are being followed in other areas of the curriculum, these should be incorporated into physical education (eg symmetry and asymmetry in mathematics can be practically applied in gymnastics or dance).
2. Teaching 2.1. Have a critical understanding of the most effective teaching, learning and behaviour-management strategies, including the use of PPA to provide opportunities for all pupils.	• Planning is detailed and demonstrates progression. • Team teaching and lesson observations have a clear focus on observations and target setting. • Discussions with teachers and pupils ascertain what the pupils have learnt as a result of the teaching, and evaluations are made as to whether this is appropriate. • A range of appropriate resources is used within lessons.	• A shared understanding of effective teaching should be developed through structured CPD. Refer to: ▪ *The Reality of High Quality Physical Education: The Crucial Role of Leadership* (afPE, 2008a) • PESS professionals should be encouraged to team teach and observations of lessons should be part of the ethos of the school. For principles of lesson observation, criteria for judgements and feedback, see:

Criteria All leaders in physical education should:	Evidence What does it look like?	Exemplification – Practical Examples Ideas for implementation
	• Time is used effectively within lessons. • Leader's own teaching is evaluated with a view to improvement. • Good practice is shared with all PESS professionals. • Clear learning objectives are shared with pupils. • Teachers have high expectations of their pupils. • Teachers have excellent knowledge and understanding of physical education. • Teachers use a range of teaching approaches and allow for pupils' preferred learning styles. • Teachers are motivating and engaging with high expectations so that pupils are appropriately challenged to succeed. • Teachers build upon pupils' prior knowledge and attainment so they can make good progress and achieve according to their ability.	■ *Appendix 12: Protocols for Observing Lessons* ■ *Appendix 13: Evaluation of Teaching* ■ *Appendix 15: Examples of Lesson Proformas.* • Where funding is provided for cover, some should be used to develop the above. • Teachers should meet the full range of pupils' needs by: ■ setting suitable learning challenges ■ responding to pupils' diverse needs of gender, cultural backgrounds or ethnicity, pupils with SEN or EAL ■ overcoming potential barriers to learning and assessment (ie pupils with disabilities and/or SEN). Refer to: ■ *Appendix 5: The NCPE's Principles for Inclusion* ■ *Success for All: An Inclusive Approach to PE and School Sport* (DfES, 2003) ■ 'Primary and Secondary Inclusion Development Programme – Supporting pupils on the autism spectrum' (DCSF, 2009) ■ 'Meeting The Needs of Muslim Pupils In State Schools' (Birmingham CYPF/Birmingham University, 2008) ■ *Appendix 22: Inclusion Spectrum for PESS.* • Teachers should ensure that activities are differentiated (using STEP), teaching styles are varied and activities are performed alone, in pairs, in small groups or in teams (large-sided teams are not acceptable).

Criteria All leaders in physical education should:	Evidence What does it look like?	Exemplification – Practical Examples Ideas for implementation
		For varying teaching styles and their inclusion in planning documents, see: ▪ *Appendix 10: The STEP Process* ▪ afPE website ▪ *Appendix 7: Teaching Styles and Preferred Learning Styles* ▪ *Appendix 8: How Teaching Styles and Preferred Learning Styles Can Be Addressed in Planning Documents.* • Using core tasks from QCA schemes of work to establish a baseline at the start of a unit, then revisiting the core task at the end of the unit, will help teachers to assess the progress of pupils, see: ▪ *Appendix 7: Teaching Styles and Preferred Learning Styles* ▪ *Every Child Matters: Measuring Moments of Progress and Inclusive Assessment* (afPE, 2007a) ▪ QCA/DfES website for schemes of work. • Teachers should use a range of explanations, questions, discussions and demonstrations so that new ideas and concepts are clearly understood by all pupils.
3. Assessing, monitoring and giving feedback 3.1. Develop colleagues' use of assessment for learning as part of their teaching in order to diagnose and meet pupils' needs through setting appropriate challenges.	• Teachers' planning includes learning objectives against which the pupils can be assessed. • Team teaching and lesson observations have a focus on the assessment and monitoring of pupils' progress. • Discussions with teachers and pupils ascertain what pupils have learnt and if they know where they go next and how to get there.	• Through CPD, teachers should understand what 'assessment for learning' means in physical education. Refer to: ▪ *Assessment for Learning in Physical Education* (afPE, 2005). • Plan for improvement, progress and attainment using QCA core tasks to establish a baseline so that appropriate tasks are planned and, if necessary, adapt or modify the tasks.

Criteria All leaders in physical education should:	Evidence What does it look like?	Exemplification – Practical Examples Ideas for implementation
	• Thorough and accurate assessment informs pupils of what they have achieved and how to improve. • Pupils are guided to assess work themselves. • Pupils make good progress as a result of effective teaching	See: ■ *Every Child Matters: Measuring Moments of Progress and Inclusive Assessment* (afPE, 2007a) ■ QCA/DfES website for schemes of work. • Teach and assess for improvement, progress and attainment by using plans, talking with pupils, asking questions and giving constructive feedback in order to support pupils' self-assessment when considering what needs to be improved and what new tasks to set. • Review for improvement, progress and achievement by helping pupils to review and reflect on their progress, judging whether they are getting close to achieving expectations and deciding what to do next.
4. Reviewing teaching and learning 4.1. Develop systems to ensure that colleagues are given opportunities to review the effectiveness of their teaching and its impact on pupils' progress, attainment and well-being.	• Data from SSPs and LA is used to share good practice. • Assessment records clearly show what pupil progress has been achieved and what areas require development. • DVD evidence is used. • Lesson observations have an agreed focus and are followed by constructive feedback, where strengths are recognised and areas for improvement are identified. • Feedback forms are used to identify areas for improvement, and discussions and agreements are undertaken to discover how this will be achieved.	• It is important to establish clear criteria when making judgements about high quality. These should focus on 'Achievement and Standards' and 'Personal Development and Well-Being', see: ■ *Appendix 2: Making the High Quality Connection and The 10 High Quality Outcomes Posters* ■ *Appendix 13: Evaluation of Teaching.* • Key sources of evaluating teaching and learning should include: ■ lesson observation ■ learners' written work ■ results and assessments ■ discussions with learners ■ observation of extra-curricular activities ■ observation of coaches and ASL.

Criteria All leaders in physical education should:	Evidence What does it look like?	Exemplification – Practical Examples Ideas for implementation
		See:
		- *Appendix 12: Protocols for Observing Lessons*
		- *Appendix 14: Suggested Questions to Ask When Sharing Lesson Observations*
		- *Appendix 15: Examples of Lesson Observation Proformas*
		- *Appendix 16: Feedback Proforma*
		- *Appendix 4: Best-practice Guidance on the Effective Use of Individual and Agency Coaches.*
		• Use information from the SSP/LA to build a picture of standards across groups of schools so that comparisons can be made. Use some of the 12 days of paid cover to visit other schools and/or attend network meetings of partnership schools to help develop opportunities to moderate judgements.
		• Use records from teachers in the school to demonstrate progress year on year, including planning and reviewing.
		• When giving feedback on lesson observations identify clear priorities for improvement with action plans that have timescales, see:
		- *Appendix 16: Feedback Proforma*
		- afPE website for NCfCPD opportunities.
		• Ensure that networking/staff meetings have effective teaching as a focus.

Criteria All leaders in physical education should:	Evidence What does it look like?	Exemplification – Practical Examples Ideas for implementation

5. Learning environment
 	
5.1. Establish and promote a purposeful and safe learning environment complies with current legal requirements, national policies and guidance on the safeguarding and well-being of pupils.
 	
5.2. Identify and establish the use of opportunities to personalise and extend learning through out-of-school contexts.
	• Records of all qualifications and CRB checks confirm appropriate expertise of all PESS staff.
	
	• Policies identify organisation and procedure in physical education.
	
	• Risk-management records are updated regularly and risk assessment is continuous and ongoing.
	
	• All PESS professionals are aware of risks attached to all activities, resources, environments and facilities, and of their general and specific responsibilities.
	
	• Details of pupils attending OSHL are recorded.
	
	• Opportunities and a directory of appropriate clubs in the community are promoted.
	
	• Good staff commitment to, and competence in, promoting health and safety is evident.
	
	• Child-protection issues are robust.
		• A copy of *Safe Practice in Physical Education and School Sport* (afPE, 2008b) should be used as definitive guidance in conjunction with the LA. This should be readily available for all teachers and ASL.
		
		• CRB checks should be in place and up to date, see:
		
		  ▪ CRB website.
		
		• ASL should undertake a physical-awareness course and teachers made aware of their duties and responsibilities when working with ASL. See:
		
		  ▪ *Appendix 4: Best-practice Guidance on the Effective Use of Individual and Agency Coaches*
		
		  ▪ *Adults Supporting Learning (including Coaches and Volunteers): A framework for development* (afPE/sports coach UK, 2007)
		
		  ▪ NCfCPD opportunities on afPE website.
		
		• Well-structured opportunities for OSHL should either enhance, enrich or enable curriculum opportunities be open to all, see:
		
		  ▪ *Appendix 21: Primary Playgrounds Development/ Sporting Playgrounds Poster*
		
		  ▪ PESSYP strategy (DCMS/QCA, 2004).
		
		• Develop school-to-club links through the SSP – the partnership should develop and maintain a list of approved clubs in the community.

6. Team working and collaboration 6.1. Promote collaboration and work effectively both as a team member and	• Good links with parents and outside agencies are evident. • Records of meetings are meticulous and up to date. • Discussions with teachers and ASL are recorded.	• Provide regular updates and CPD opportunities, which are linked to priorities identified individually and collaboratively. • Performance management should be structured and understood by

Criteria All leaders in physical education should:	Evidence What does it look like?	Exemplification – Practical Examples Ideas for implementation
manager of physical education. 6.2. Be part of, or work closely with the leadership team taking a role in developing, implementing and evaluating policies and practice with colleagues in physical education. 6.3. Be able to work effectively within the SSP team.	• Collaboration with all PESS personnel provides enough time, teachers and coaches, space and equipment to enable learners to learn and achieve. • Learners are listened to and action is taken on what they say. • Parents/carers are involved and informed, and what they say is listened to and acted upon.	all. Refer to: • TDA Performance Management web page. • Create opportunities to share and disseminate good practice through team teaching, networks and meetings. • Establish support mechanisms for NQTs/new teachers/ASL. All should be allocated a mentor. • Roles and responsibilities should be clearly stated and agreed by all. The physical education handbook should list these and be updated at least once every two years. • Ensure a culture of openness, honesty and respect is fostered and nurtured. • Arrange regular meetings with school sport coordinator (SSCO)/partnership development manager (PDM) and other schools in the partnership. • Explain the value of PESS to learning, health and well-being in a way that learners, teachers, parents and governors can understand.

a practical guide to achieving excellence and high quality leadership in primary physical education

Teacher Resource Signposts

afPE (2005) *Assessment for Learning in Physical Education*. Leeds: Coachwise Business Solutions. ISBN: 978-1-902523-79-2

afPE (2007a) *Every Child Matters: Measuring Moments of Progress and Inclusive Assessment*. Leeds: Coachwise Business Solutions. ISBN: 978-1-905540-40-2

afPE (2008a) *The Reality of High Quality Physical Education: The Crucial Role of Leadership*. Leeds: Coachwise Business Solutions. ISBN: 978-1-905540-56-3

afPE (2008b) *Safe Practice in Physical Education and School Sport. Leeds: Coachwise Business Solutions*. ISBN: 978-1-905540-54-9

afPE/sports coach UK (2007) *Adults Supporting Learning (including Coaches and Volunteers): A framework for development*. Leeds: Coachwise Business Solutions. ISBN: 978-1-905540-28-0

Birmingham CYPF/University of Birmingham (2008) 'Meeting the Needs of Muslim Pupils in State Schools', www.afpe.org.uk/public/downloads/muslim_guidance_nov08.pdf

DCMS/DfES (2004) 'High Quality PE and Sport for Young People', www.teachernet.gov.uk/_doc/6254/HighQualityLeaflet.pdf

DCSF (2009) 'Primary and Secondary Inclusion Development Programme – Supporting pupils on the autism spectrum', http://nationalstrategies.standards.dcsf.gov.uk/node/165037

DfES (2003) *Success for All: An Inclusive Approach to PE and School Sport* (CD-ROM). DfES: 054 2003

QCA (1999) 'Statutory Inclusion Statement', http://curriculum.qca.org.uk/key-stages-1-and-2/inclusion/statutory-inclusion-statement/index.aspx

TDA (2007) 'Professional Standards for Teachers', www.tda.gov.uk/standards

Websites

Association for Physical Education
www.afpe.org.uk

Criminal Records Bureau
www.crb.gov.uk

Department for Children, Schools and Families
www.dcsf.gov.uk

Healthy Schools
www.healthyschools.gov.uk

National College for Continuing Professional Development
www.afpe.org.uk/public/ncfcpd_courses.htm

Qualifications Curriculum Authority
www.qca.org.uk

QCA Schemes of Work
www.standards.dfes.gov.uk/schemes3/

TDA Performance Management
www.tda.gov.uk/teachers/performance_management.aspx

Appendix one
Key References to Support *A Practical Guide to Achieving Excellence and High Quality Leadership in Primary Physical Education*

a1

afPE (2005) *Assessment for Learning in Physical Education*. Leeds: Coachwise Business Solutions. ISBN: 978-1-902523-79-2

afPE (2006a) *A Guide to Self-review in Physical Education*. Leeds: Coachwise Business Solutions. ISBN: 978-1-902523-98-9

afPE (2006b) *Self-evaluation in Physical Education: Developing the process*. Leeds: Coachwise Business Solutions. ISBN: 978-1-905540-06-8

afPE (2007a) *Every Child Matters: Measuring Moments of Progress and Inclusive Assessment*. Leeds: Coachwise Business Solutions. ISBN: 978-1-905540-40-2

afPE (2007b) *Professional Development Record*. Leeds: Coachwise Business Solutions. ISBN: 978-1-905540-39-6

afPE (2008a) *The Reality of High Quality Physical Education: The Crucial Role of Leadership*. Leeds: Coachwise Business Solutions. ISBN: 978-1-905540-56-3

afPE (2008b) *Safe Practice in Physical Education and School Sport*. Leeds: Coachwise Business Solutions. ISBN: 978-1-905540-54-9

afPE (2008c) 'Simple Guide to Completing your Self Evaluation Form', www.afpe.org.uk/public/downloads/SEF_guide.doc

afPE/sports coach UK (2007) *Adults Supporting Learning (including Coaches and Volunteers): A framework for development*. Leeds: Coachwise Business Solutions. ISBN: 978-1-905540-28-0

baalpe (2003) *Achieving Excellence*. Leeds: Coachwise Business Solutions. ISBN: 1-902523-57-1

Birmingham CYPF/University of Birmingham (2008) 'Meeting the Needs of Muslim Pupils in State Schools', www.afpe.org.uk/public/downloads/muslim_guidance_nov08.pdf

CfSA Primary Subjects (2008) 'Physical Education: Making every child matter', www.afpe.org.uk/public/downloads/CfSA_PE_Apr08.pdf

CfSA (2009) 'Physical Education: Learning outside the classroom', www.afpe.org.uk/public/downloads/Pri_sub_4.pdf

DCMS/DfES (2004) 'High Quality PE and Sport for Young People', www.teachernet.gov.uk/_doc/6254/HighQualityLeaflet.pdf

DCSF (2006) 'Learning Outside the Classroom', www.lotc.org.uk/getmedia/b84de479-7990-482c-a17b-b527ae7d32f2/LOtC-Leaflet.aspx

DCSF (2007) 'The Children's Plan: Building Brighter Futures', www.dcsf.gov.uk/childrensplan/downloads/The_Childrens_Plan.pdf

DCSF (2009) 'Primary and Secondary Inclusion Development Programme – Supporting pupils on the autism spectrum', http://nationalstrategies.standards.dcsf.gov.uk/node/165037

DENI/ETI (2008) 'A Common Framework for Inspection', www.etini.gov.uk/common_framework-2.pdf

DfES (2003) *Success for All: An Inclusive Approach to PE and School Sport* (CD-ROM) DfES 054 2003

DfES (2004) 'Every Child Matters – Change for Children' www.everychildmatters.gov.uk

Estyn (2002) 'The Common Inspection Framework for Education and Training in Wales', www.estyn.gov.uk/publications/lea_services_in_wales_2007.pdf

Kolb, A. and Kolb D. A. (2001) 'Experiential Learning Theory Bibliography 1971–2001', www.haygroup.com/tl/Downloads/LSI_Bibliography_06.pdf

Mosston, M. and Ashworth, S. (1986) Teaching Physical Education. Columbus, Ohio: Merrill Pub Co. ISBN: 978-0-675204-59-0

Ofsted (2005) 'The Common Inspection Framework for inspecting education and training', www.ofsted.gov.uk/Ofsted-home/Forms-and-guidance/Browse-all-by/Other/General/Common-Inspection-Framework-for-inspecting-education-and-training

QCA (1999) 'Statutory Inclusion Statement', http://curriculum.qca.org.uk/key-stages-1-and-2/inclusion/statutory-inclusion-statement/index.aspx

QCA (2005) 'Do you have high quality PE and sport in your school?', www.qca.org.uk/libraryAssets/media/self_evaluation_guide.pdf

TDA (2007) 'Professional Standards for Teachers', www.tda.gov.uk/standards

TDA (2009) 'Experiential Learning', www.pezone.co.uk

Websites

Association for Physical Education
www.afpe.org.uk

Coachwise 1st4sport
www.1st4sport.com

Council for Subject Associations
www.subjectassociations.org.uk

Criminal Records Bureau
www.crb.gov.uk

Department for Children, Schools and Families
www.dcsf.gov.uk

Department of Education, Northern Ireland
www.deni.gov.uk

Healthy Schools
www.healthyschools.gov.uk

HM Inspectorate for Education and Training in Wales
www.estyn.gov.uk

HM Inspectorate of Education in Scotland
www.hmie.gov.uk

a practical guide to achieving excellence and high quality leadership in primary physical education

Learning Outside the Classroom
www.lotc.org.uk

National College for Continuing Professional Development
www.afpe.org.uk/public/ncfcpd_courses.htm

National College for School Leadership
www.ncsl.org.uk

National Curriculum
http://curriculum.qca.org.uk/

National Occupational Standards for Supporting Teaching and Learning in Schools
www.tda.gov.uk/support/NOS/supporting.aspx

NSPCC Child Protection in Sport Unit
www.nspcc.org.uk/inform/cpsu/cpsu_wda57648.html

Office for Standards in Education, Children's Services and Skills
www.ofsted.gov.uk

PESS strategy for Wales
www.wales.gov.uk/about/departments/dcells

PESSYP Professional Development Programme
www.youthsporttrust.org/page/cpd/index.html

Physical Education Initial Teacher Training and Education
www.peitte.net

Qualifications Curriculum Authority
www.qca.org.uk

QCA Schemes of Work
www.standards.dfes.gov.uk/schemes3/

Teachernet
www.teachernet.gov.uk

Training and Development Agency for Schools
www.tda.gov.uk

TDA Performance Management
www.tda.gov.uk/teachers/performance_management.aspx

Welsh Assembly Government
www.wales.gov.uk

These posters can be found on the *A Practical Guide to Achieving Excellence and High Quality Leadership in Primary Physical Education* CD-ROM, titled *Appendix 2: Making the High Quality Connection.pdf* and *Appendix 2: The 10 High Quality Outcomes.pdf*.

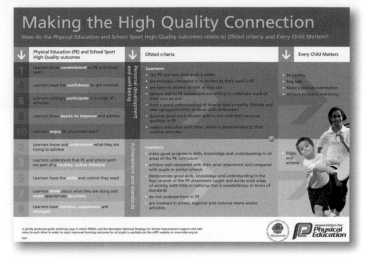

Appendix 2: Making the High Quality Connection.pdf
(Created by afPE and DCMS)

Exemplar of Appendix 2: The 10 High Quality Outcomes.pdf
(Created by DCMS and QCA)

Appendix three

Executive Summary of the Rose Review of the Primary Curriculum 2009

The full *Executive Summary of the Rose Review* can be found on the *A Practical Guide to Achieving Excellence and High Quality Leadership in Primary Physical Education* CD-ROM, titled *Appendix 3: Executive Summary of the Rose Review of the Primary Curriculum 2009.pdf*

Appendix 3: Executive Summary of the Rose Review of the Primary Curriculum 2009.pdf

Where the term 'school' is used, this includes SSPs, community learning partnerships and others working on behalf of the school. Where the term 'lesson' is used, this includes sessions delivered before school, during lunchtimes and after school.

Extensive guidance exists on the employment, deployment and management of coaches in PESS, such as that provided by the DCSF, NSPCC CPSU and afPE. However, best practice is not always evident in schools. This brief checklist was created by a group of afPE members during a workshop at the 2007 conference as support for head teachers and others in schools who manage the employment and work of coaches.

Head teachers and other managers of coaching support staff are strongly advised to follow the guidelines below.

1. Safe Recruitment

a. Arrange a face-to-face interview with all coaches to confirm their identity using original documents (passport, driving licence, recent service provider bill confirming current home address).

b. Check CRB enhanced disclosure. See original; decide if portability applies and is acceptable; check with original responsible authority and establish whether additional information is on the CRB form. If so, request a new certificate from the coach to access the additional information. If no response is received to enquiry or information is withheld, a new disclosure certificate is essential.

c. Check qualifications. See originals; accept Level 2 award as normal baseline qualification for each activity the coach is expected to teach, only diverting from this standard if the coach is observed prior to acceptance and demonstrates exceptional coaching qualities and is working towards a Level 2 qualification; refer to the higher level teaching assistants (HLTA) standards for your baseline (www.hlta.gov.uk).

d. Check training undertaken and experience of working with children and young people (eg child protection workshops).

e. Explore motivations to work with children and attitudes towards children and young people.

f. Check reference(s). Investigate any gaps in coaching employment and any conditional comments in the reference.

g. Check with relevant national governing body (NGB) that coach is currently licensed to coach (qualification cannot be rescinded, but NGB licence to coach can be if any poor practice or abuse issues have arisen).

h. Ensure correct employment status and employment rights are known to the coach. Provide written summary/include in contract, as appropriate.

i. Ensure coach is fully aware of insurance provision and what aspects he/she needs to provide for him/herself (according to employment status) re:

- employers' liability (compulsory) – legal liability for injuries to employees (permanent/temporary/contracted for services) arising in course of employment

- public liability (essential) – legal responsibility for 'third-party' claims against the activities of the individual/group and legal occupation of premises

- professional liability (desirable) – legal cover against claims for breaches of professional duty by employees acting in the scope of their employment (eg giving poor professional advice)

- hirers' liability (desirable) – covers individuals or agencies that hire premises against any liability for injury to others or damage to the property whilst using it

- libel and slander insurance (optional) – cover against claims for defamation (eg libellous material in publications)

- personal injury – accidental bodily injury or deliberate assault (desirable) – arranged by the individual or the employer

- miscellaneous – a variety of types of insurance, such as travel (compulsory or required) or motor insurance (compulsory – minimum of 'third party') – check personal exclusions and excesses the individual carries.

j. Set out a clearly defined role, identifying any limits of responsibility, lines of supervision, management and communication, specialist expertise needed (eg children with individual special needs) and ensure they are appropriately qualified/experienced to undertake the role.

k. Determine an agreed period of probation and monitor the coach's performance and attitude closely during this period.

l. If an agency coach, check that all of the above has been addressed by the agency or by the school before the coach begins work.

m. Agree an appropriate induction package that must be fulfilled.

2. Induction

a. Head teacher or their representative to present coach with a summary of relevant school policies and procedures, including risk assessments, emergency evacuation, referral and incentives, behaviour management, first aid, child-protection procedures and something about the ethos of the school – how staff work with children and young people (such as looking for success in young people, rewarding achievement).

b. Identified member of staff to manage induction into school procedures who will:

- arrange meeting with SENCO (and class teacher[s] as appropriate) or other nominated personnel (eg SSCO) for specific information about pupils

- monitor and assess the competence of the coach through observations and discussions with pupils and other staff

- determine the coach's role in contributing to the overall assessment of pupils.

3. Qualifications, Experience and Qualities Necessary for a Coach to Work Alone

a. Level 2 award is the normal baseline qualification for each activity the coach is expected to teach. Divert from this standard only if the coach is observed prior to acceptance, demonstrates exceptional coaching qualities and is working towards a Level 2 qualification.

b. Check previous experience in working with small/large groups.

c. Check behaviour management skills.

d. Check:

- quality of relationships – the way the coach cares for and respects pupils, is an appropriate role model and promotes the ethos of school

- developing knowledge of the pupils – their levels of confidence, ability, individual needs, medical needs and behaviour

- pupil management – how they match pupils' confidence, strength and ability in pair and group tasks, maximise participation, have strategies for effective pupil control and motivation, apply the school's standard procedures and routines (eg child protection, emergency action, jewellery, handling and carrying of equipment)

- knowledge of the activities – appropriate level of expertise to enable learning to take place in the activities being delivered, use of suitable space for the group, differentiated equipment, differentiated practice, evident progression and application of rules

- observation and analytical skills – providing a safe working and learning environment, ability to identify faults and establish strategies for improvement.

4. Day-to-day Management of Coach

a. Check the coach has received a summary of school and subject procedures and understands what is required (including clear guidelines in relation to handover of responsibility at the start and end of lessons/sessions).

b. Ensure the coach receives relevant information on pupils/groups (eg illness, family bereavement, behaviour issues).

c. Monitor promptness.

d. Establish regular review and evaluation of coach's work.

e. Determine who assesses pupils' work.

f. Ensure coach is supported, valued and is accepted as a member of staff.

g. Monitor dialogue and relationship between class teacher and coach.

5. Monitoring Quality and Effectiveness

a. Ensure direct monitoring of coach for agreed period – use criteria set out in section 3 on previous page.

b. Set up continual indirect monitoring to ensure pupils make progress and enjoy lessons/sessions.

c. Ensure pupils are engaged in consistent high quality, challenging and stimulating activities that support them to achieve their potential, not just activities that keep them 'busy, happy and good' pupils that do not demonstrate high quality – see High Quality Physical Education (DCMS/DfES 2004).

6. Identification and Provision of Continuing Professional Development

a. Evaluate coach's abilities against HLTA standards.

b. Arrange attendance on afPE/sports coach UK ASL induction course.

c. Agree essential qualifications and desirable qualifications – plan and provide for personal development programme beyond NGB coach qualifications to enable coach to proceed from emerging to established, and advanced rating.

7. Dealing with Inadequate Performance by the Coach

a. Proactively monitor coach's work as set out in section 5 (above).

b. Where performance is inadequate and poses a health-and-safety risk to the pupils or has the potential to impact on their welfare, intervene immediately. Where performance is technically inadequate, review situation with the coach after the lesson.

c. Agree and provide supportive continuing professional development to improve inadequate aspects of performance.

d. Monitor for improvement.

e. Where little or no improvement occurs, terminate short-term contract or initiate competency procedures if longer-term contract.

f. Where necessary, terminate longer-term contract where competence does not improve.

The NCPE sets out the following three main principles for inclusion that should underpin planning and provision for all pupils.

1. Suitable inclusive learning challenges should involve tasks and activities that:

   - teach knowledge, skills and understanding in ways that suit pupils' abilities (choose from earlier or later key stages)

   - are sufficiently flexible to meet the cultural background of all pupils (eg travellers, refugees, asylum seekers, pupils with long-term medical problems)

   - have a much greater degree of differentiation for pupils whose attainments fall significantly below the expected levels at a key stage

   - provide suitably challenging work for pupils whose attainments significantly exceed the expected level.

2. Responding to pupils' diverse learning needs should provide opportunities for success for all pupils, including:

   - boys and girls

   - pupils with SEN

   - pupils with disabilities

   - pupils of different ethnic groups, including travellers, refugees and asylum seekers

   - pupils from diverse linguistic backgrounds.

3. Overcome potential barriers to learning and assessment for individuals and groups of pupils by:

   - helping with communication, language and literacy

   - developing understanding

   - planning for full participation, ie:

     - using specialist aids/equipment

     - providing support from adults or peers when needed

     - adapting tasks and/or environment

     - providing alternating activities where necessary

   - managing behaviour, ie:

     - setting realistic demands

     - using positive behaviour management

     - giving pupils the chance to develop cooperative skills

     - teaching pupils to value and respect each other

     - encouraging/teaching independent learning

     - teaching essential safety

- managing emotions

- providing support to pupils with disabilities by providing adapted, modified or alternate activities

- providing support to pupils with EAL by developing the spoken word and ensuring effective opportunities for talk.

Note: Teachers also need to take account of pupils' religious and cultural beliefs and practices through provision of appropriate physical activity and learning opportunities.

a practical guide to achieving excellence and high quality leadership in primary physical education

The National Curriculum for physical education is an entitlement for all pupils between the ages of 5–16 years and, although some might not attain the age-related levels, it is important the principles below are included.

Learning Across the Curriculum

All pupils are entitled to access:

- **Personal, social, health, citizenship education (PSHCE)**

  This involves:

  - gaining the confidence and responsibility to make the most of their abilities
  - preparing to play an active role as citizens
  - developing a healthy, safer lifestyle
  - developing good relationships and respecting differences
  - creating a breadth of opportunities.

- **SMSC**

  This involves:

  - spiritual, ie having a sense of achievement
  - moral, ie ensuring fair play and sporting behaviour, and accepting authority
  - social, ie engaging in cooperative activities, taking responsibility, being loyal, engaging in teamwork and participating in social activities
  - cultural, ie understanding their own and others' cultures.

- **Key skills**

  These include:

  - communication, ie verbal and non-verbal
  - application of numbers, ie data analysis, measuring and recording
  - ICT, ie use of digital recording equipment
  - working with others, ie in a variety of roles, cooperating with others
  - improving own learning and performance, ie recognising what they do well and what needs to be improved
  - problem solving, ie different ways of approaching a task and changing approach if necessary.

- **Other aspects**

  These include:

  - thinking skills, ie critical evaluations of aspects of performance and the expression of ideas and opinions
  - work-related learning, ie in organisational roles
  - education for sustainable development, ie the understanding of a healthy lifestyle.

- **Use of language**

  This involves:

  - speaking, ie the precise and cogent use of language
  - listening, ie listening to others and responding and building on their ideas and views constructively.

- **Health and safety**

  This consists of understanding hazards, risks and risk control and how to:

  - recognise hazards, assess them and take steps to control them for themselves and others
  - use information to assess immediate and cumulative risk
  - manage the environment to ensure health and safety for themselves and others
  - explain the steps they take to control risks.

Appendix seven
Teaching Styles and Preferred Learning Styles
(see Mosston and Ashworth, 1986)

a7

The following table represents a worthwhile model in relation to the link between teaching style and individual pupils' preferred way of learning, however, there is a need for equal emphasis on the 'how' of pupil learning and the need for teachers to adopt sympathetic teaching styles.

It is important teachers become aware of the fact their preferred teaching style may clash with a reasonable percentage of preferred learning styles in any one group, and with many aspects of safety. However, consideration should be given to selecting teaching styles in relation to individual pupils' needs, their preferred learning styles and to the desired learning outcome. Several styles, therefore, may appear in a single lesson.

Preferred Learning and Teaching Style	Essential Characteristics	Likely Objectives	Focus
Command or direct	• All decisions made by teacher. • Learners do as they are told. • Class responds as a group.	• Conformity to a single standard of performance. • Efficiency in the use of time to acquire skills. • Safety and discipline.	Motor development
Practice	• Most decisions made by teacher. • Learners make some decisions. • Practice time set by teacher who can support individuals.	• Improve skills. • Make learners aware of link between time allocation and quality of outcome. • Help learners judge level of performance.	Motor development
Reciprocal	• Planned by teacher, executed by learners. • Learners work in pairs, one as a teacher and one as a learner, then exchange roles. • Clear criteria given. • Pupils hold responsibility.	• Engage pupils in social situations. • Develop communication skills. • Develop skills of observation, listening, analysing. • Raise awareness of others, patience and tolerance. • Provide for maximum feedback from learners.	Social and motor development

Preferred Learning and Teaching Style	Essential Characteristics	Likely Objectives	Focus
Self-check	• Planned by teacher with clear criteria. • Learners check own performance. • Decisions made by pupils based on criteria.	• Help learners assess their own performance. • Help personal development (eg honesty and ability to be objective). • Help learners identify strengths and weaknesses.	Personal and motor development
Inclusion	• Planned by teacher. • Learners check own performance starting at their level and progressing appropriately. • Set tasks highlight individual progress.	• Maximise involvement at appropriate individual levels • Accommodate individual differences. • Help learners set realistic targets. • Enable all learners to succeed.	Personal and motor development
Guided discovery	• Teacher plans target and systematically leads learners to 'discover' the target. • Open-ended questioning is fundamental. • Planning appropriate steps to discovery is critical. • Redirection of learners who are off-target is essential.	• Engage learners in a convergent process of discovery. • Develop sequential discovery skills and consequences of action. • Develop patience whilst progressing through skilful matching of response to questions and stimuli.	Cognitive and motor development
Problem solving	• Teacher presents questions or problem situation and pupils invited to discover solutions. • Learners in small groups to encourage shared thinking. • Learners contribute to decisions at all stages as their response may determine their next move.	• Develop problem-solving skills. • Develop understanding of an activity structure through the search for a solution. • Develop the ability to verify solutions. • Encourage independent thinking. • Promote learners' confidence in their own ideas and responses.	Cognitive, social, motor and personal development

a practical guide to achieving excellence and high quality leadership in primary physical education

Preferred Learning and Teaching Style	Essential Characteristics	Likely Objectives	Focus
Individual	• Learner designs and plans the programme. • Teacher proposes the focus/content and approves programme.	• Encourage independent planning and assessment under guidance. • Reveal level of understanding through application. • Encourage persistence in completing a programme. • Promote self-confidence.	Cognitive, personal and motor development
Learner initiative	• Learner selects content and plans and designs programme with teacher's approval. • Learner executes programme and submits evaluation to teacher.	• Encourage and develop independence. • Display understanding through selection and application. • Encourage acceptance of personal responsibility. • Develop self-confidence.	Cognitive, personal and motor development
Self-teaching	• The learner is both teacher and learner and works fully independently.		Cognitive, personal and motor development

The following examples use the QCA scheme of work:

Invasion Games – Units 23/24, Years 5/6

The overall aim in invasion games is for pupils to cooperate with teammates, start to use tactics to outwit opponents and compete fairly as individuals and as team members.

In this unit the pupils should learn to*:

- develop the range and consistency of their skills

- devise and use rules

- use and adapt tactics in different situations

- recognise which activities help their speed, strength and stamina

- recognise when speed, strength and stamina are important in games

- explain their ideas and plans

- recognise aspects of their work that need improving.

> * These are measurable objectives against which pupils are assessed at the end of the unit.

Teachers should employ a range of teaching styles and strategies (see Kolb, 1984) to ensure learners are given plenty of opportunities to learn by:

- feeling, ie applying 'concrete experience'

- watching, ie 'reflective observation'

- thinking, ie 'abstract conceptualisation'

- doing, ie 'active experimentation'.

Core tasks

A core task in Years 5/6 (QCA units 23/24) can be used at the beginning of a unit for the teacher to assess pupils' ability and to plan further expectations and learning that enable most pupils to:

- play invasion games with some fluency and accuracy, using a range of throwing and catching techniques

- find ways of attacking and defending

- know the rules and understand how strength, stamina and speed can be improved through playing invasion games.

They should be able to undertake an appropriate warm-up and to watch and describe others' performance as well as their own in order to suggest practices that will help them and others to play the game better. After the unit is completed (in 12–18 weeks), the core task can be used again to assess what progress has been achieved.

ICT: A video camera can be used to collect evidence at the start and end of the unit and pupils can use the footage to make judgements about their progress.

An example of how a teacher might use one of the Year 5/6 core tasks:

The desired outcome is a game where the ball is passed to a nominated player in the end zone of the pitch, who then must shoot to score a goal.

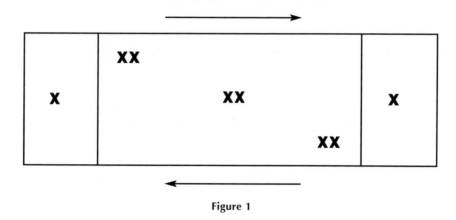

Figure 1

Teaching and learning style: Problem solving

- Teacher presents the problem/task and asks the pupils to discover the solution.

- Pupils are organised into groups to encourage shared thinking.

- Pupils contribute to decisions at all stages as their response may determine the next move.

1. Teacher divides pupils into groups of six and allocates an area (see Figure 1) to each group.

2. Each group to decide what the focus of the game is (using 'thinking' or 'abstract conceptualisation'), ie hockey, netball, football, basketball, and select appropriate equipment.

3. Teacher tells the pupils what the desired outcome of the game should be and gives them a set time to devise a game that meets the criteria. This gives them an opportunity to 'feel' (concrete experience) what the game might look like.

4. As they are playing, the teacher asks them to 'watch' (reflective observation) what is working and what isn't, and start to develop ideas about how they can improve the game (eg what rules they might introduce). This gives the pupils an opportunity to reflect and start to develop abstract thoughts/ideas, ie 'thinking' (abstract conceptualisation).

5. When they have made a group decision as to which idea(s) they should use, the pupils put them into practice, ie 'doing' (active experimentation).

6. The cycle is continuous and the teacher will set new outcomes to move the pupils forward into the next stage of 'feeling' (concrete experience) a different invasion game.

Teaching and learning style: Guided discovery

- Teacher plans a target and systematically leads the learners to discover the target.

- Questioning by the teacher is fundamental to this style.

- The choice of appropriate steps in the discovery process is critical to success.

- Redirection of pupils who go off target.

1. The pupils are divided into groups of six and allocated a space, see Figure 1.

2. Teacher gives the pupils an outline of the game:

   - Netball-type game

   - Play four attackers v two defenders

   - Pass the ball between the attackers to get it to player in zone who then shoots at the goal.

3. Pupils play the game, giving them the opportunity to 'feel' (concrete experience) what it's like and to 'watch' (reflective observation) what is and isn't working.

4. Teacher uses specific closed/open questions to guide pupils towards introducing additional rules, for example, no moving when in possession of the ball or no contact with other players. In conjunction with the teacher, the pupils are encouraged to 'think' (abstract conceptualisation) and develop abstract ideas.

5. Pupils then put their ideas into practice, ie 'doing' (active experimentation).

6. The cycle is continuous and as pupils develop the game, they move through to the next stage of 'feeling' (concrete experience) a game with a different focus, guided by the teacher.

The following examples illustrate how an individual session might be planned following on from the core task. Both examples are taken from TDA online materials to support physical education CPD and are planned using the same QCA unit of work, but with different planning styles.

Example One: Invasion Games – Units 23/24, Years 5/6

Focus of Lesson	Activity or Main Content of Session	Experiential Learning Opportunities and Teaching and Learning Styles	Inclusion	Resources
Sending and receiving in netball-type activity (measurable learning goals highlighted in bold). **Skills and processes** Pupils should learn: 1. How to explore and investigate ideas in order to understand physical skilfulness in games activities and acquire and develop the skills of sending and receiving in netball. 2. How to be able to create and develop their skills through practising on their own and with each other thus developing their personal	**Warm-up** Building on prior learning, ask pupils what activities should be in a warm-up for invasion games. Combine stretching, stamina and skills development into a warm-up routine. **Development** In pairs with ball passed between them; try different distances – near together and then further apart. • How does this change the way of passing? Teach how to position bodies for receiving and passing the ball. Introduce rule that you can't receive pass in same space – you must move after sending the ball, but not when in possession.	Reflective observation (watching) Active experimentation (doing) Concrete experience (feeling) **Teaching and learning style:** Guided discovery Concrete experience (feeling) Reflective observation (watching) Abstract concept (thinking) then active experimentation (doing) **Teaching and learning styles:** Practice and self-check Abstract concept Experimentation Reflective observation Concrete experience	Peer support – less able pupils are paired with more able Pupils paired/grouped according to ability, and space allocated made smaller (for the more able) or bigger (for the less able). Foam balls for the less able Hoops for targets	White board Video camera and playback facility, if required Variety of netballs

Focus of Lesson	Activity or Main Content of Session	Experiential Learning Opportunities and Teaching and Learning Styles	Inclusion	Resources
and social skills – work together to improve throwing and catching techhniques in attack and defence. 3.How to participate positively with each other when devising a game or practice – set up a mini netball-type game with clear rules and strategies. 4. How to reflect and evaluate on their work in order to improve their choices and decision making – decide what works and what doesn't and make changes in order to improve.	Join pupils with another pair and continue with same activity and same rules, passing to each pupil in turn. Pupils should evaluate how this changes the activity and check each other's performance. Introduce concept of attack and defence 3 v 1. • How does this work in practice? • What adjustments do you have to make? **Game** Staying in same groups, get the pupils to devise a mini game with a scoring system. • What are the rules? • How does it work – do the rules or the game need to be changed? **Plenary or post-session assessment** Refer to outcomes on whiteboard – use questions to establish understanding. Pupils check and reflect on their own performance against the outcomes and identify which areas need further practice. **Cool-down** Pupils to devise stretches.	**Teaching and learning styles:** Guided discovery and self-check		

Example Two: Invasion Games – Units 23/24, Years 5/6

Focus of lesson: Sending and receiving in a netball-type activity.

Aims:

- To develop the pupils' ability to think about how the skills of sending and receiving are essential in invasion games (ie 'perception continuum').
- To support the pupils' ability to develop skills of sending and receiving in a netball-type activity (ie 'processing continuum').

Learner objectives*:

- To appreciate the need for a warm-up and cool-down for a netball-type activity.
- To be aware of the need for rules of their game.
- To acquire and develop skills and techniques in order to play a simple netball-type game.
- To review and evaluate what works and what doesn't.
- To develop control and fluency through practising sending and receiving.
- To start to develop strategies and tactics for basic attacking and defending.

Opportunities to enhance:

- Using a variety of teaching strategies to ensure different learning needs are catered for.
- Ensuring pupils are given opportunities for reflective observation and active experimentation when practising the skills in netball.
- Using effective grouping/pairing strategies to address different abilities.
- Use of STEP (see *Appendix 10: The STEP Process*) to ensure that all pupils differing needs are catered for.

Personal and social skills developed*:

- Pupils' ability to work cooperatively in pairs and in group work.
- Pupils' ability to discuss and share ideas.
- Pupils' ability to respond to challenges set by the teacher and come up with solutions.
- Pupils' ability to manage risk and stay safe.

'Skills for life' or key skills developed:

- Pupils' ability to be refective learners.
- Pupils' ability to be team workers through positive relationships.
- Pupils' ability to be effective participators by developing their skills and performance.
- Pupils' aspirations, by them taking responsibility and making the most of opportunities.

Taking part in group discussion*:

- Contribute to decisions about adapting the task when working in pairs and groups.
- Help to decide what works well and what doesn't, and identify appropriate changes.
- Take turns at the leadership role within the group.
- Contribute to the group discussion when devising the mini-game.

> * These are measurable objectives against which the pupils can be assessed during the session.

Time	Teacher Plan	Learner Activity	Resources	Reflecting on Practice
10 mins	**Introduction and warm-up** **Teaching and learning style:** Guided discovery Using both closed and open questions, establish what the pupils learnt and can remember from previous lessons – if necessary, get pupils to demonstrate. Use a whiteboard to outline the objectives for the session – link them to prior learning and make sure pupils understand what they will learn in this session. If video footage is available, use this to explain or start the discussion. Building on prior learning, ask pupils what should be in a warm-up for invasion games – teacher ensures safe practice through appropriate questions to guide the pupils.	Explain or show their understanding of different ways of sending and receiving. Working in pairs, devise a warm-up routine which combines stretching, stamina and skills development.	Whiteboard Video camera and playback facility, if required Balls, if needed	Teacher uses assessment for learning process throughout the session: Plan for improvement, teach and assess for improvement and finally review for improvement to inform next stage of planning. Pupils have opportunities to 'think' and 'reflect'. Those that need to can demonstrate – ie 'doing' and 'feeling'. Peer support – less able pupils work with more able.
20 mins	**Development** **Teaching and learning styles:** Practice and self-check Explain the task, then select pupils to demonstrate to ensure understanding. Use questions to ascertain when to use different passes (eg chest pass or overarm pass). Teach how to position bodies for receiving and passing the ball. Introduce the rules that you can't receive a pass in	In twos with the ball passed between them, try different distances, ie close together and then further apart. Ask: How does this change the way of passing? Discuss, reflect or experiment. Join two pupils with another pair	Variety of types of netballs, including foam balls Bibs	Pupils paired/grouped according to ability and space allocated is made smaller (for the more able) or bigger (for the less able). Foam balls for the less able. Inclusion is by outcome – pupils decide who passes and determine the distances between them. Choice of ball type made by pupils with

a practical guide to achieving excellence and high quality leadership in primary physical education

Time	Teacher Plan	Learner Activity	Resources	Reflecting on Practice
	same space and you must move after sending the ball, but not when in possession. Ask: How does this affect the game? Introduce the criteria for pupil evaluation. Introduce the concept of attack and defence, ie 3 v 1. Ask: • How does this work in practice? • What adjustments would you have to make?	and continue with same activity and same rules passing to each in turn. Pupils should evaluate how this changes the activity and to check each other's performance. Pupils choose a defender and take turns at defending. Ascertain which strategy for defending works best and why?	Variety of types of netballs, including foam balls Bibs	guidance from teacher. The whole cycle of experiential learning is used in this activity – they start with the concrete experience, but observe and reflect continuously as they play, developing ideas and then experimenting by using them ('diverging–assimilating–converging–accommodating').
15 mins	**Game** **Teaching and learning style:** Guided discovery and self-check Staying in same groups get the pupils to devise a mini game with a scoring system. Use questions to establish: • What are the rules? • How does the game work? • Do the rules or the game need to be changed? • How do you score? Ask pupils to use the passes they have practised.	Working cooperatively, the pupils talk, discuss and try out ideas and concepts to devise a game (ie they decide whether it is 2 v 2 or 3 v 1). Building on the skills and ideas they have used during the development phase of the lesson, pupils now create and develop a game. In order to make improvements to their game they reflect and evaluate using set criteria.	Bibs Variety of balls Hoops for targets	Pupils stay grouped according to their ability – this can be changed during the game activity if necessary if the teacher adapts or modifies the activity. The learning starts with an abstract concept which leads to experimentation (ie converging) to see if their game is effective. This is followed by reflective observation to improve or revise the game, moving to the final version of the game, which is a concrete experience (ie diverging).

Time	Teacher Plan	Learner Activity	Resources	Reflecting on Practice
5 mins	**Plenary or post-session assessment** **Teaching and learning style:** Self-check Refer to the outcomes on whiteboard – use questions to establish pupils' understanding. **Cool-down** **Teaching and learning style:** Learner intiative Ask questions about appropriate cool down linked to previous learning.	Pupils check and reflect on their own performance against the outcomes. Pupils work on their own, devising stretches and calming activities.		This supports personal development of pupils in terms of honesty and objectivity. It also helps pupils to recognise their limitations (ie reflective observation). This encourages independent thinking and also allows the pupils to display their understanding of cool down (ie accommodating).

The aim of the STEP process is to ensure that all pupils with differing needs are catered for. Teachers should use the STEP approach when planning their sessions, ie:

- **S**pace – change the space to either make the task harder or easier (eg standing further apart makes the game easier to play whereas standing nearer together makes it harder).

- **T**ask – change or adapt the task (eg when practising in pairs, introduce a bounce pass to make it easier or change the rules in the game to make it easier or harder).

- **E**quipment – change equipment (eg use different balls such as foam balls or lighter balls for the less able and standard netballs for those of higher ability).

- **P**eople – change the pairs or the groups to cater for different abilities (eg sometimes working in mixed ability groups/pairs or working in similar ability groups/pairs with teacher supporting some pupils).

> **Note:** There is detailed information about the STEP process on the afPE website, www.afpe.org.uk

Key for adaptation

It is important to link invasion-type games, for example ask: How is this game similar to that one? For example, hockey and soccer have very similar strategies and tactics with the only real difference being the equipment, whilst netball and basketball require similar skills.

Assessment of pupil improvement, progress and attainment

Assessment is inextricably linked to planning (see references to assessment in planning examples in appendix nine) as the teacher needs to be very clear where the pupils are in their learning, where they need to go and how best to get there.

The first part of the planning process is to:

- establish a baseline to reaffirm where pupils are in their learning (this can be done using the core tasks outlined in the QCA schemes (see www.standards.dfes.gov.uk/schemes3)

- have clear expectations of what the pupils are capable of achieving

- plan appropriate learning goals

- share the learning goals with the pupils

- be ready to adapt, modify or change the plans and expectations, if the pupils need to be more challenged or less challenged.

Once the planning is done, the next stage is to use it to teach the pupils and use the learning goals in the planning to set appropriate tasks. In order to support pupils in self-assessment, maintain ongoing dialogue with them by asking questions to ascertain their views, and giving constructive feedback. This will help them consider what needs to be improved as well as planning and setting new tasks.

For the assessment process to be effective, it is important that the teacher regularly takes stock by helping pupils review and reflect on their performance and progress so that judgement can be made as to whether the learning goals set at the beginning have been achieved in order to decide what to do next.

The school used in this case study is a community primary school in London with approximately 500 pupils, 70% of whom speak EAL. Every member of the school is encouraged to contribute towards a purposeful secure environment where everyone feels valued and is encouraged to maximise their potential.

The school extended its opportunities for experiential learning in physical education through lunchtime activities. In order to raise standards in physical education, the school linked what was happening within the curriculum to activities outside the curriculum. Because the majority of pupils needed to improve their English, as well as their standards in physical education, the school decided to 'learn by doing' would be the most effective way of achieving both.

The experiential cycle of learning outlined by Kolb (1984) was adopted as a whole-school strategy and, as a result, pupils became familiar with learning in this way across all subjects. In other words they were always given time to 'get a feel' (ie concrete experience) for the activity/skill they were to learn, then time to watch and reflect (ie reflective observation) on their experience, which resulted in them thinking (abstract conceptualisation) of new ideas or changes they would like to try. After a time of experimenting (active experimentation) with their ideas/concepts they would then return to the concrete experience and actually 'feel' the improvement they had achieved.

To make better use of playtimes the playground was zoned into different learning spaces, one of which was designated for team games and each class was allocated this space for one day each week. All decisions about the allocation timetable were determined by the school council so the pupils themselves had 'ownership' of the area.

Year 4

By the end of Year 4, pupils were expected to be able to:

- refine their play and cooperate with others to increase their skills and control

- begin to create their own rules, and to use more complex tactics and strategies

- be given more responsibility for their own learning and be enabled to make more confident and informed choices about their health and environment

- through their involvement in a range of social interactions, learn to take account of other people's feelings

- have opportunities to increasingly participate in the life of the school and start to think about opportunities that might be available in the community.

Note: These are criteria the teacher can use to build up an accurate picture of pupils' progress across the curriculum as well as in games activities.

During the autumn term the school decided to block the two lessons per week into a half-term unit of invasion games – in other words, from September to the end of October, the pupils focused only on invasion games in curriculum time (approximately 12–18 hours).

The pupils planned and designed the lunchtime programme with approval from their teacher. They organised their own groups in order to encourage shared thinking, and at all stages pupils contributed to decisions that determined the next move. Participation was voluntary, but over the half-term 80% of the class became involved in some way or another, taking on different roles in rotation, which provided opportunities for leadership, officiating, organising and playing. Pupils were also encouraged to develop skill-based resource cards that could be used to practise running, dodging, throwing and catching skills, all of which are crucial elements of invasion games.

Each week they practised the game they had performed in the lesson (ie applying concrete experience or feeling) and added or changed rules or equipment (active experimentation as a result of ideas developed from reflective observation). Time was allocated after their lunchtime session to reflect upon and evaluate what they had done and start to develop ideas to actually experiment with in their next lesson.

Standards right across the school improved significantly as a result of this experiential learning approach and pupils' attitudes to learning became more positive because they were involved at all stages, which also contributed to the improvement in standards.

Health and Safety Issues

Experiential learning or 'learning by doing' must ensure risk management is central to safe practice. Children simply can't be sent off to do an activity unless they know how to manage the risks and learning to do this is an essential part of the experiential cycle. It is recommended that teachers use *Safe Practice in Physical Education and School Sport* (afPE, 2008) as a first point of reference when developing a risk-management strategy.

The three dimensions that need to be considered when looking at the risk factor are:

- the people involved in the activity (eg in the invasion games examples given in this paper appropriate grouping/pairing of pupils is important to ensure they 'stay on task' and work within the rules; teachers should always stay on the periphery so that all pupils are within their sight

- the context in which the activity takes place (eg the areas allocated for the practices/games must be large enough and with enough space between them to minimise the risk of collisions etc)

- the organisation of the activity (eg pupils must warm up before the activity and be aware of working within their own space to avoid contact with others).

Principles

- Communication with staff should be purposeful and productive.

- Evaluations of lessons should be objective and presented honestly, clearly and frankly.

- All staff should be treated with courtesy, respect and sensitivity.

- Teachers' confidence should be built up and mutual respect established.

- All efforts should be made to minimise the stress on teachers being observed.

- Observers should ensure that they understand what a teacher is doing and why.

- Findings on lessons should be shared with teachers in a helpful way.

- Confidentiality of information.

- Teachers' work should not be discussed within earshot of others.

- Concerns to be discussed with SMT should be discussed with the teacher beforehand.

Fitness for purpose

- Why is the lesson being observed?

- Why has this particular lesson been selected?

- What is the focus of the lesson observation?

Procedures

Read or collate 'evidence' in advance of and during the lesson and ask:

- What are the objectives for teaching and learning?

- How will you assess to what extent they have been achieved?

- The role of the observer, his/her place in the room and his/her contribution (or not) to the lesson must be agreed.

- The proforma to be used must be agreed.

- Collate evidence for the lesson (eg lesson plan, place of lesson in module/scheme).

- Courtesies must be observed.

- Time and venue for feedback must be agreed and understood.

- The audience for outcomes/dissemination must be clear and understood.

- Feedback must be verbal and written.

- Copies of feedback to others (eg staff development officer) must be agreed beforehand.

Conduct of observer

- Be unobtrusive.
- Talk to learners about their work without disrupting lesson.
- Avoid approaching the teacher during the lesson.
- Ensure you observe all the different ability groups within the class.
- Avoid making contributions to the lesson, unless prearranged with the teacher.

Sharing observations

- Establish a relaxed professional atmosphere.
- Focus on impact of teaching on learners' achievement and personal development.
- Judgements should be clear and accurate.
- Judgements must be fair and backed up with evidence.
- Evaluations must recognise strengths as well as weaknesses.
- The focus should be on the lesson, not the person.
- Opportunities for discussion should be given.
- You should not overwhelm the teacher with too many weaknesses.
- You should give helpful advice that will lead to action.
- You should acknowledge improvements as soon as possible after the initial observation.

a practical guide to achieving excellence and high quality leadership in primary physical education

Teaching and Learning	Effectiveness of Teaching and Learning in Meeting the Needs of the Full Range of Learners
You should evaluate: • How well the teaching meets the needs of the full range of learners, and course requirements. • The suitability and rigour of assessment in planning, learning and monitoring learners' progress. • The diagnosis of, and provision for, individual learning needs. • Where appropriate, the involvement of parents and carers in pupils' learning and development.	• Do teachers/ASL have high expectations and engender a love/passion for the subject? • Do they have excellent knowledge of the subject pedagogy? • Is there regular assessment of learners and rigorous use of assessment data, including that from previous schools, to inform planning? • Are there effective plans for progression and continuity within the structure of the scheme of work? • Are there clear learning objectives that are shared with learners? • Do teachers/ASL use an appropriate range of strategies and materials to support learning for all learners? • Do they use questioning and exposition to establish links with prior learning in order to develop and check current learning? • Is there a focus on developing core skills and ICT within the subject, alongside individual and collaborative study and problem-solving skills? • Do they use opportunities to develop social, spiritual, moral and cultural awareness? • Is there use of a range of appropriate resources within lessons? • Do teachers/ASL make effective use of time within lessons? • Do teachers/ASL evaluate their own teaching with a view to improvement? • Are there opportunities to share good practice with colleagues?

Open questions:

- Which part of your teaching do you enjoy most?
- How would you describe your experience of...?
- What would you like to gain from this?
- What do you think would be the best way to take this forward?

Probing questions:

- In what way?
- How did you feel when you had completed the lesson?
- What makes that part of the job more interesting/more satisfying/difficult?
- Will you expand on that a little?
- Why is that important?
- What makes it helpful/difficult to work in that way?

Reflective questions:

- So you are saying that...?
- Are you telling me that...?
- If I were to summarise what you have told me, would I be right in saying...?

Closed questions:

- Have you used this computer program often?
- What resources do you use for...?
- Where did you find this information?

Closed questions that lead to specific information or a 'yes' or 'no' reply may need to be followed up with more open questions, for example:

- Have you used this method before? (Closed)
- What did you think of it? (Open)
- What are the advantages of using this one? (Open)
- Are there any disadvantages? (Closed)
- How did you overcome them? (Open)

Multiple questions:

- Will you tell me what you've done best and what you need to improve on?

- Are you happy with the agenda? Would you like to add something or do you think we should approach it differently?

> **Note:** These types of questions are best avoided as they are often confusing and usually only one question gets answered.

Leading questions:

- I'm sure you can see the advantages of this, can't you?

- Don't you think that would be a good idea?

You are likely to get a positive response whether the teacher agrees with you or not, so it is important to follow up with an open question:

- I'm sure you can see the advantages, can't you? What are the advantages?

Example One (as used by Ofsted)

EVIDENCE FORM											
Inspector		URN			Observation Time			Observation Type			Lesson Analysis Discussion/ Observation
Year Group(s)		Grouping			Subject Codes			Number in Class Boys/Girls			
Teacher Status	Q U T S G N A	Support Teachers/ Assistants	SEN	T	S	EAL	T	S	Oth	T	S	Inspector's EF No	

Focus (ie main purpose of the inspection activity)

Evidence and evaluation

Summary

Judgement on the overall quality of the lesson (Leave blank when not a lesson.)	1 = Outstanding 4 = Inadequate	☐

Use for grades, or tick to indicate evidence on:

Standards	Progress	Personal development	Teaching	Curriculum	Care Guidance and Support	Leadership and Management

Particular evaluations related to safety, health, enjoyment, contribution to the community or economic well-being.

Example Two (simplified version of Ofsted form)

School:	Date:

Teacher:

Class:

Activity:

Context:

What Made the Lesson Good	Issues to Focus on to Improve Teaching and Standards

Pupil standards:

Ofsted Grade

Judgement on the overall quality of the lesson (Leave blank when not a lesson.)	1 = Outstanding 4 = Inadequate	

Use for grades, or tick to indicate evidence on:						
Standards	Progress	Personal Development	Teaching	Curriculum	Care, Guidance and support	Leadership and Management

Particular evaluations related to safety, health, enjoyment, contribution to the community or economic well-being.

Observer: Teacher:

Date: Focus:

Time:

Contextual information:

Strengths:

Areas for development:

Teacher's comments:

Agreed actions and timescales:

Other comments:

Appendix seventeen

a17

Directing Improvement and Promoting the
Well-Being of Pupils in Physical Education
Through High Quality Care and Education

Questions to Ask	Judgements and Evidence
What monitoring and evaluation procedures do you have in place?	
How do you measure improvement?	
To what extent are core tasks used to determine progress?	
To what extent is pupils' progress discussed at staff meetings? To what extent is it a standing item on the agenda?	
How often do you meet and talk with parents?	

Questions to Ask	Judgements and Evidence
To what extent are the procedures for assessment understood by all, including pupils?	
To what extent are pupils involved in their own assessment?	
To what extent are expectations clear and shared by all?	
To what extent do assessment procedures address the processes in knowledge, skills, and understanding?	
To what extent do you use assessment data to inform planning and practice?	

a practical guide to achieving excellence and high quality leadership in primary physical education

Questions to Ask	Judgements and Evidence
How do you monitor and develop staff?	
To what extent is team teaching used effectively? What benefits does it have?	
To what extent is there a mentoring system, particularly for new colleagues?	
To what extent do all staff have the opportunity to observe each other using clear criteria agreed prior to the observation?	
To what extent are there systems in place to share good practice both within your school and with other schools?	
How are professional development needs identified (and met) through appraisal/performance management reviews?	
To what extent are clear expectations and constructive working relationships established between all staff?	
To what extent are 'experts' such as LA/afPE officers, advanced skills teachers and teacher advisers used effectively?	
To what extent are child protection procedures clear and understood by all, including ASL?	

Appendix twenty

Monitoring the Efficiency of How Equipment, Learning Resources and Accommodation are Managed to Ensure Pupils are Well Taught and Protected

a20

Questions to Ask	Judgements and Evidence
To what extent are sufficient resources available for pupils to have sufficient practice in order to make progress and improve?	
How does your management of resources ensure that they are readily accessible for curriculum and OSHL?	
To what extent are equipment, resources and accommodation suitable for all pupils, including those with disabilities and special needs?	
How do you ensure that systems in place support staff to use different equipment appropriately in order to meet the needs of all pupils	
Is there a named person who has responsibility for monitoring the condition, safety and sufficiency of the equipment?	
How do you ensure that systems in place allow the available accommodation to be used effectively?	
How do you ensure that accommodation is allocated in such a way that pupils have the best opportunity to learn?	
To what extent does long-term planning take into account the times when space/accommodation is not available?	
What opportunities exist for pupils to use other facilities outside school whenever possible?	
How are staff deployed so that their strengths are recognised and used effectively?	

a practical guide to achieving excellence and high quality leadership in primary physical education

The *Primary Playgrounds Development/Sporting Playgrounds Poster* can be found on the *A Practical Guide to Achieving Excellence and High Quality Leadership in Primary Physical Education* CD-ROM, titled *Appendix 21: Primary Playgrounds Development/Sporting Playgrounds Poster.pdf*

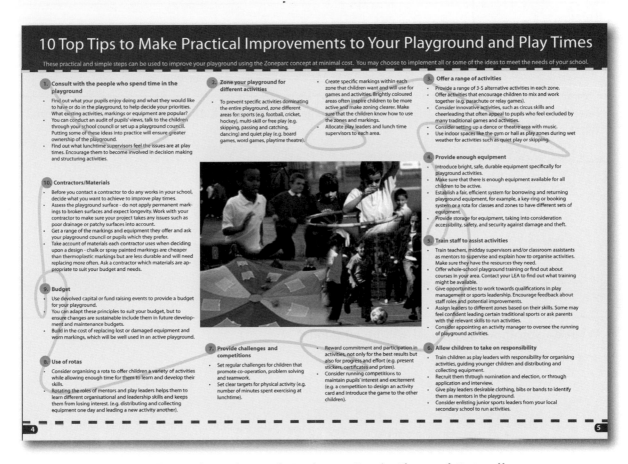

Appendix 21: Primary Playgrounds Development/Sporting Playgrounds Poster.pdf
(Created by DfES)

Example One: PESS CPD Audit of Needs

Name:	
Role:	
Class:	

Based on your self-review, performance management feedback and only lesson observation, what are your CPD needs?

What do you think the impact will be on pupils?

What are your physical education CPD needs?

a practical guide to achieving excellence and high quality leadership in primary physical education

Example Two: PESS CPD Audit of Needs

Areas of Expertise and Core Skills	Context and Range In Which Skills Will Be Applied	Evidence of Current Skills (Where have you applied the skills identified? What evidence can show that you are skilful in the area of expertise?)	Area(s) and Skills for Development

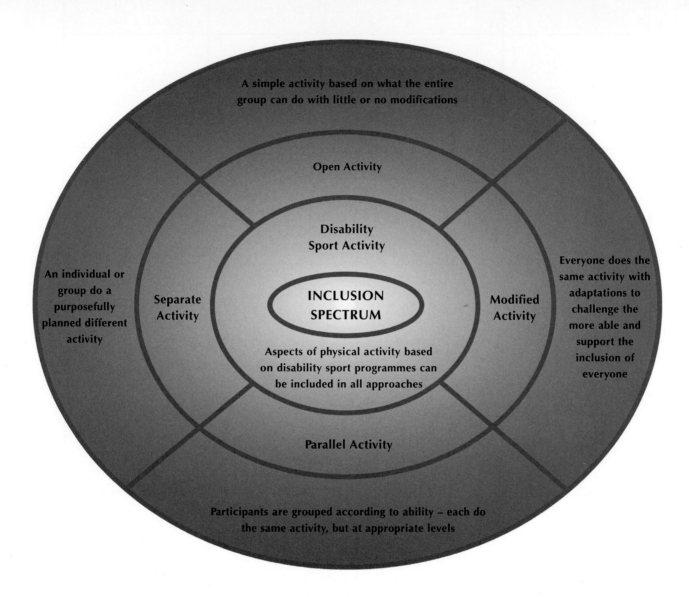

A simple activity based on what the entire group can do with little or no modifications

Open Activity

Disability Sport Activity

INCLUSION SPECTRUM

Aspects of physical activity based on disability sport programmes can be included in all approaches

An individual or group do a purposefully planned different activity

Separate Activity

Modified Activity

Everyone does the same activity with adaptations to challenge the more able and support the inclusion of everyone

Parallel Activity

Participants are grouped according to ability – each do the same activity, but at appropriate levels

Inclusion Spectrum for PESS

Adapted by Pam Stevenson and Ken Black for the Youth Sport Trust